THE ALDERSON STORY

My Life as a Political Prisoner

I Speak My Own Piece: *Autobiography of the 'Rebel Girl'*

The
ALDERSON STORY

My Life as a

Political Prisoner

by Elizabeth Gurley Flynn

NEW YORK
INTERNATIONAL PUBLISHERS

Dedication

*To my dear and devoted sister, Anne K. Flynn ("Kathie"
to family and friends)—who died February 24, 1962, who was
my faithful correspondent and visitor; who made all arrangements to publish my first book, while I was in prison; who
wrote articles, made speeches, and helped to carry on a campaign for my release; and who by her courage, cheerfulness,
understanding and great sense of humor, helped to make my
time in Alderson more bearable and my whole life, at all
times, easier and happier—I dedicate this book, to her memory, in love and sorrow.*

ISBN: 0-7178-0002-4
Library Of Congress Catalog Card Number: 63–10863
Printed in the United States of America

PUBLISHER'S NOTE

Elizabeth Gurley Flynn died on September 5, 1964, at the age of 74, a year and a half after this book was first published. The 28 months she was a "resident" of the Federal Women's Reformatory at Alderson, West Virginia—from January 1955 to May 1957—no doubt affected her already failing health. She epitomizes an entire epoch of militant labor history, from her first soap-box speech in 1906, through the great strike struggles and mass defense campaigns, until her own imprisonment under the thought-control Smith Act and then her public activity on behalf of other imprisoned Communist leaders. She remained to the last "The Rebel Girl" of Joe Hill's song.

The injustices and suffering of prison life, about which she writes with such perception and human understanding in this book, are now brought to wide public attention by the revolts which have been sweeping the prison system. Having spent most of her life defending the victims of class justice as it operates in the courts and in the prisons and as a political prisoner herself, what she has to say here will strike a deeply responsive cord among the active "politicals" of the present generation and their defenders. In a broader sense, most of the Blacks, Puerto Ricans and other oppressed minorities who fill our prisons are also political prisoners, having been victimized by the same poverty and racism on the outside which subject them to a double sentence on the inside.

Many of the demands advocated in this book have recurred again and again in the petitions and declarations of the prison rebels, but deepened and enhanced by the new awareness of the intense social crisis reflected in the prison rebellions. The social injustice and racism which characterize the entire judicial and prison system are now pilloried in the great nationwide and worldwide movement for the freedom of Angela Y. Davis and all political prisoners. Elizabeth Gurley Flynn would have fully appreciated and welcomed with her fiery spirit this new chapter in the fight for social justice.

—JAMES S. ALLEN

January 1972

Contents

[1]

"For Teaching and Advocating"

On a hot morning in June 1951, the bell of our apartment on East 12th Street in New York City rang insistently. A knock came on the door, too soon for anyone to have climbed the three flights of stairs after we had pressed the button to open the downstairs door. There were two groups apparently, one already waiting outside our apartment. My young niece was preparing for school. My sister Kathie was cooking breakfast. She opened the door and I heard her scream out indignantly.

Three FBI agents, two men and a woman, roughly pushed their way past her. They stated they had a warrant for my arrest. I took the document and read it. It was for alleged violation of the infamous Smith Act. "For teaching and advocating the violent overthrow of the government, when and if circumstances permit," it said.

The phone rang and Kathie answered. It was from a friend down the street. "Yes, I know," Kathie said, "they are here too." I dressed in the presence of the jittery young woman, who came uninvited into my bedroom. I was allowed time for one cup of coffee. I tried to reassure my family in parting, "Don't worry. This is a long range proposition." It was. It did not end until July 1957, when I came out of prison and was finally free of parole restrictions.

The raiding party escorted me downstairs to a waiting car.

It was early, few neighbors were on the street. At the FBI headquarters, then located in the Federal Court House at Foley Square, a number of my comrades, also under arrest, were assembled. We were given coffee and we sat there, awaiting the completion of the round up of our group, which the press unflatteringly called "the second string Communists." Finally, when 16 were present, we were registered and fingerprinted. By permission, I telephoned my sister, watched by one of the arresting officers, who then telephoned his wife. He had told us this was not his regular line of work. It was amusing how identical were our words. We both said: "Don't worry. Everything is alright." That he had to go forth at dawn to arrest a Communist apparently had his family as much in a dither as my arrest had mine.

We were next taken into a courtroom to be arraigned and have bail set. The formalities were brief. While we were in the courtroom, our venerable crippled comrade, Israel Amter, who was then over 70 years old, was brought in. Murmurs of "Shame!" were heard, as he painfully hobbled down the middle aisle, leaning on the arm of his wife. He had been dragged from a nursing home in upstate New York, over the protests of the attendants. He was released in the custody of a lawyer until $500.00 could be posted for bail later. For the rest of us bail was extremely heavy. We were loaded into patrol wagons. The men were handcuffed in pairs, including Jacob Mindel and Alexander Trachtenberg, both over seventy, and taken to the Federal House of Detention on West Street.

We four women were taken to the Women's House of Detention, on Greenwich Avenue. Marian Bachrach, now dead, was one. She was severed later from our trial to undergo an operation for cancer; in spite of that, she was subsequently tried with a third group and finally acquitted. Claudia Jones, a young Negro woman, was with us. She served a year in prison and was then deported to England. Betty Gannett and I were the other two. Marian's bail was placed immediately by her mother. She was our "glamor girl." She wore a pale purple summer suit, a little hat with purple flowers, and carried a square basketpurse with a nosegay on top. The inmates gazed at her and exclaimed, "Isn't she cute!"

The Civil Rights Congress Bail Fund put up bail for all of us except Marian and one man whose family placed his. But the Fund's trustees were involved in a hassle with the federal authorities, who were demanding the names of all persons who had loaned money to the bail fund. They refused to divulge the names, determined to protect people from the rampant McCarthyism of the period. As a consequence, Abner Green, Dashiell Hammett, W. Alphaeus Hunton, and Frederick V. Field, the four trustees, were jailed for contempt of court. In reprisal against them, all bail bonds from the Fund were cancelled and 14 of us were sent back to jail. The two who were free constituted themselves a committee to raise new bail for the rest.

It was a lengthy and tedious procedure. Persons offering the bail were compelled to take the witness stand and swear that the money belonged to them, and even to produce bank records to prove it. The government lawyers and the judges were determined to prevent any money coming from the Bail Fund. But many good people, indignant at such persecution, came forward, drew money from their savings accounts, took funds out of safe deposit boxes and borrowed money on personal property to give us our freedom. My excessively high bail of $25,000 was put up by Grace Hutchins, an elderly woman of courage and integrity. When the prosecutor asked her the source of her money she replied, "I inherited it." He sought to discredit her: "The record shows you were in China. What were you doing there?" She replied quietly, "I was a missionary." He hastily accepted the bail.

The atmosphere at that time was heavy with McCarthyism, the cold war, and the Korean war, which affected all Smith Act cases. Our arrests had immediately followed the Supreme Court decision which upheld the constitutionality of the

Smith Act and rejected the appeal of the first group of Communist leaders in what was called the Dennis case. They had been arrested in 1948. William Z. Foster and I were the only two of the Communist Party's National Board of 13 who were not involved in this trial. He had been severed because of illness. But he remained under indictment and on bail until his death on September 1, 1961. As the only woman member of the Board I felt quite embarrassed and at a loss to explain why I was not arrested with my co-workers. I felt discriminated against by Uncle Sam!

Later during our trial it became evident that there was legal strategy behind the government's action. I had been purposely left out of the first case and held over for the second trial, as a link between the two groups of defendants, who were charged in the same alleged conspiracy. My presence apparently was calculated to help the government establish continuity of the conspiracy. It was called the Flynn case, which did not mitigate my indignation against the whole legal chicanery. As soon as all defendants were free on bail we faced another difficulty. We were unable to secure lawyers to represent us. After defense counsel in the first case had been threatened with jail and disbarment, no one wanted to defend Communists in a Foley Square trial and we could hardly blame them.

The treatment in the first Smith Act trial accorded both defendants and their lawyers by Judge Harold R. Medina, who presided, was insulting and abusive. His attitude was so prejudicial that he was more prosecutor than judge. From the outset he made plain his dislike of the defendants and contempt for the attorneys. He bullied witnesses, took over cross-examination from the prosecutor, and made a fair trial impossible. After the jury brought in their verdict of guilty he thanked them profusely and then said, "I now have some unfinished business." He proceeded to lash out in a bitter attack on the defense lawyers and sentenced all of them, including Eugene Dennis, who acted as his own attorney, to jail for contempt of court. Later, he was severely criticized by some Justices of the U.S. Supreme Court. But at the moment we suffered the direct consequences. Lawyers were loath to go into the same court to suffer similar indignities.

In attempting to overcome this situation we had some interesting experiences. We sent letters to tens of lawyers in New York and elsewhere. In the main, the replies were courteous. A few were curt, but all declined to help us. Defendants personally interviewed many lawyers. One group went to see Harold Ickes, who had been Secretary of the Interior under F. D. Roosevelt. He gave them a friendly reception, but he was too old to undertake a trial. However, he sent us a fine letter expressing his vigorous views on our right to have counsel, recommending that other lawyers take over our case, and authorizing us to use the letter. As our trial date approached we went into court before Judge Sylvester J. Ryan to present our problem. He wasn't much help. First he called in a large number of lawyers who were known as liberals, and attempted to appoint them. It was interesting to see how they got off the hook! They were all busy, had important cases, were already court appointed, were ill, going for an operation next week, and what have you. Privately, many told us they had nothing against us, but Foley Square? No, thanks.

Next Judge Ryan drew up a list of lawyers whom he undertook to contact personally and urge to take our case. They were criminal lawyers, with one or two exceptions publicly identified with notorious underworld characters. One had defended a group of Brooklyn police accused of grafting on the underworld. Another had defended smugglers accused of bringing gold into the country. At the top of the list was a Mr. Wolf, the attorney for Frank Costello. We had often seen Mr. Costello in court, a quiet little man, neatly dressed, who is reputed to be a top gangster, but who could easily be mistaken for a lawyer or courtroom spectator.

Simon W. Gerson was then one of our defendants, but was subsequently acquitted by the judge because the government never mentioned his name in their entire case. He and I decided to see Mr. Wolf, and went to his uptown office. It was sedately furnished, with British courtroom prints on the walls and we were greeted by a demure secretary. Mr. Wolf was mayor of the Long Island town where he lived. He had often been in court during the first Smith Act trial, had heard Eugene Dennis speak and was much impressed by him. He was well-informed on the issues relative to the Smith Act. But he made his figure prohibitive.

We visited an ex-district attorney in Brooklyn, who had never heard of the Smith Act. He said impatiently, "So what's the evidence?" When we replied, "Books," he asked incredulously, "Would I have to read books?" One of our amused committee said: "Oh, yes, several hundred on politics, economics, world history, etc." He replied scornfully: "No, thanks. I don't like books. I like to fish," and showed us out. The lawyer for the policemen flew in by plane to see us from his vacation in New England, out of respect for Judge Ryan. He was Jewish but talked with a strong Irish accent, possibly from his long association with cops, or an affectation. He too, was not interested.

The one rare exception on the list was Mr. Frank Serri of Brooklyn, an officer of the Lawyer's Guild, a fine lawyer, and a scholar. His first act after agreeing to take part in our case was to order all the works of Marx, Engels, Lenin, and Stalin, published by International Publishers. By the time we came to trial he had thoroughly familiarized himself with them. We were fortunate to thus break the ice with Mr. Serri's acceptance, and soon we had assembled a splendid team of lawyers, adding Mrs. Mary Kaufman, Mr. Thomas Wright, a Negro attorney of Washington, D.C., and Mr. John T. McTernan. After nine years of government service with the National Labor Relations Board and other Federal agencies, Mr. McTernan had distinguished himself in California as an outstanding labor, civil rights, and civil liberties lawyer.

Our trial judge was Edward S. Dimock, in every possible

way different from Judge Medina. He was calm, reasonable, and courteous to lawyers and defendants. We were granted the presumption of innocence. He created a relaxed court atmosphere, allowing one defendant with ulcers to have milk brought in regularly. One of his favorite witticisms was: "Never underestimate the ignorance of the judge." His rulings were timid and cautious, but occasionally helpful. In the first case, Medina sentenced all the defendants to five years and expressed regret that he could not make it ten. In our case, Judge Dimock refused the government's insistent demand for five-year sentences and graded them to three, two, and one year. He had already released two of the defendants for lack of evidence, the first in any Smith Act case. During the trial he permitted me to go to Atlanta Federal Penitentiary with one of our lawyers, John McTernan, to consult with my dear friend, Eugene Dennis. I cannot speak for all my co-defendants, but I have a kindly feeling for "our little judge." Now that he is retired I may say so, I hope, without bringing governmental wrath on his head.

[2]
The Women's House of Detention

It had a swanky-sounding address, 10 Greenwich Avenue. A tall building, with fancy outside ornamentation, it could easily be mistaken for an apartment house, except for its long narrow heavily-screened windows. For many years Jefferson Market had been located there, adjoining a police court with a clock tower. It was at one time the notorious night court, where prostitutes were taken directly from the streets by plainclothes detectives who often had propositioned them.

The market was torn down to build the jail. The old clock tower has long been threatened with demolition. A community movement fought successfully to save it, as a landmark.

A less suitable location for a penal institution could hardly be found. On one side is Sixth Avenue (struggling to be called The Avenue of the Americas); on the other side is Greenwich Avenue. Ninth Street ends on its East side and Christopher Street starts on its West side. All are busy intersections. There was a constant flow of traffic—buses, cars, trucks, and people passing on all sides, at all hours. The night noises of Greenwich Village, which apparently never goes to bed, deprived the inmates of sleep. There was singing, shouting, fighting, musical instruments—what have you. Never was there a quiet moment. Whistles came up from the streets to attract the attention of a particular inmate. Others would call her. Families, friends, sweethearts, pimps, all arranged such contacts with the women on visiting days. When we were there in 1951 proposals were voiced in the press to tear the place down. But it is still in use, an ugly house of pain and sorrow.

Inside the building pandemonium reigned supreme. The noise was deafening, from the shrill incessant chatter of the inmates, the hysterical laughter, the screams of suffering addicts suddenly cut off from narcotics, and the weeping and cursing of forlorn and desperate women, crowded together in small quarters. The majority were awaiting trial or were there during their trials, because they could not secure bail. Some stayed there for months and then were acquitted as innocent, but there was no redress. When Judge Anna Kross became Commissioner of Corrections, she found men and women in city jails who had never had a trial and had been forgotten. Some women serve sentences there up to three years. I did not ascertain on what basis they were kept in such a place, where there are no facilities for exercise or fresh air except a small wire-enclosed roof.

The cells were open, with a short curtain over the toilet as a concession to privacy. In each cell there was a narrow iron cot with a thin mattress, a covered toilet which also served as a seat before a small iron table, a washbowl, and a couple of stationary wooden hangers for clothing. The blankets were old and worn beyond all possibility of real cleanliness, though they were disinfected regularly. It was a filthy place, overrun with mice and cockroaches. The food was indescribably revolting, unfit to eat. Watery spaghetti, half-cooked oatmeal, coffee that was hardly more than luke-warm water, wormy prunes, and soggy bread baked by the men on Welfare Island, very little meat and that usually an unsightly bologna—are items I recall. There was never any fruit. Sugar and milk were scarce and both had to be bought in the commissary by inmates.

One pleasant episode lighted up our stay here. A 19-year-old Negro girl, discouraged and lonely, happened to mention that the next day would be her birthday. We bought a cake, cookies, and candies from the commissary and Betty persuaded the officer, a Negro woman, to allow us to eat last, after the other corridors had finished, so that we could give her a little birthday party. We made candles of tissue paper for the cake, covered the table as nicely as possible with paper napkins, and sang "Happy birthday." We made speeches to her and she cried with surprise and happiness. The next day we received a note from her as follows: (exact spelling)

"Dear Claudia, Betty and Elizabeth. I am very very glad for what you all did for me for my birthday. I really don't now how to thank you. I can just write what I feel on this paper. Yesterday was one of the best years of my life. I think even thou you all are Communist people that you all are the best people I have ever met. The reson I put Communist in this letter is because some people don't like Communists for the simpel reason they think the Comunist people is against the American people but I don't think so. I think that you all are some of the nces people I ever met in my hol 19 teen years of living and I will never forget you all no matter where

I be. I will always remember you Betty and Elizabeth in my prayers and I do hope our father God will help you three as well as me and everybody else. I hope you all will get out of this trouble and never have to come back in a place like this. I just can't get over yesterday. Long as I live I will never forget that I met three nice people. Well this is all I have to say except that I hope you will all go home soon. May God bless you and keep you for many more years to come. Good night. Trust in God, He will show the way. Jean." Feb. 7-1953.

While we were there at this time we were writing our final court speeches to the Judge. Naturally the inmates asked us, "What are you doing?" They insisted we read them aloud. They were an appreciative, respectful audience. Some cried with emotion and some applauded. It was very touching.

I came to know the House of Detention very well. I was in and out of it five times from 1951 to 1955, all in connection with the same Smith Act trial. I often recalled with amusement one evening in the late 1940's when I passed by the building with an Australian woman whom I had met in Paris in 1945, at the founding of the Women's International Democratic Federation. She was in New York as a representative of her country on the Women's Rights Commission of the United Nations. She asked about the building. When I told her what it was she inquired: "Have you ever been there?" When I answered, "Not yet!" she laughingly prophecied, "Don't worry. You will be." A few years later I could reply, "And how!"

In 1951 the inmates spoke with great feeling of Mrs. Ethel Rosenberg, who had been there for many months, up to a short time before we arrived. She had made a profound impression on all who met her—prisoners and guards alike. She had taken a sick prostitute into her cell and cared for her. She sang for the inmates. They said they would never forget her sweet voice singing "Goodnight Irene," a popular song of the day. Possibly she was removed because of our coming, but she was taken suddenly to the Death House in

Sing Sing prison, where she and her husband Julius were later executed on a framed-up charge of espionage. We were told when she left the House of Detention there was not a dry eye in the place.

I returned to the House of Detention during our trial in 1952 to serve two sentences of thirty days each for contempt of court. Judge Dimock ruled that they could be served concurrently. This was a penalty for refusing to identify people as Communists who were not defendants in Smith Act cases. The Fifth Amendment does not apply to voluntary witnesses. I testified for eight weeks as a defense witness. On days I was not in court I worked in the prison sewing room. I spent Christmas there. It was enlivened by the Almanac Singers serenading me from the street below. The inmates rushed to the windows, shouting, "Salvation Army!" But when they heard the words, "Open up the jail doors and throw away the key!" they cheered and said, "They must be Elizabeth's friends."

On Christmas Day I attended services in the chapel. A play depicting the nativity was performed by inmates who were serving sentences. A young prostitute, blonde and innocent looking, played the Virgin Mary. Negro women, tall and handsome, played the three kings and the wise men. The choir sang beautifully. Their sad voices in "Behold That Star!" were unforgettable.

Officers and inmates treated me courteously, as a rule. But the one in charge of the clothing room was a grim-faced old Irish woman to whom all inmates were scum of the earth. Because I had to go to court regularly, I carried on a running warfare with her not to tie my dress and coat in a bundle and throw them on the floor, her routine procedure. Only my threat to complain to the judge persuaded her to let me hang them up properly. Another Irish officer insisted on calling me Elizabeth Bentley. When I protested vigorously, "She is a stool pigeon!" she said, "Bless my soul!" and never repeated it.

One day an officer called me to the supply room. "Do you need some soap?" she asked loudly, thrusting some into my hand. Then in a low voice she said: "Elizabeth, my husband and I feel so sorry that you are here. We have heard you speak at Madison Square Garden. If you need anything tell me. But, please be careful, don't mention me to anyone." Throughout my long life I have found friends like this in a few unexpected places.

I had a couple of arguments with inmates, but none too serious. Once I astonished the women in this place of the vilest and most obscene language, by saying to a red-baiting inmate, with the deepest scorn I could command, "Don't be ridiculous." "Did you hear what Elizabeth said?" they asked. The strongest curse could not have been so startling.

On another occasion a powerful Negro woman came into my cell and looked at the material I was allowed to have under court order, to prepare for my closing remarks as counsel *pro-se*. I had acted as my own counsel during the trial. She noticed a picture of former Communist Councilman and Negro leader, Benjamin J. Davis. She said scornfully, "I come from Atlanta and he and his father are crooks." I stood up and said angrily: "I don't know anything about his father. But Mr. Davis is a friend of mine, a fine man, and in prison for fighting for the rights of people like you." She left in a huff and other Negro women rushed in to say: "Be careful Elizabeth. She's dangerous. She knocked a policeman down and took his gun away from him." But I was too angry to be frightened. Later, she returned and said: "I'm sorry, Mrs., I just wanted to see if you would speak up for your Negro friend." After that we were good friends.

The dehumanizing degradation of the House of Detention commences immediately. All your possessions are surrendered, except glasses, and one gets a receipt upon entry. But rumor had it that officers borrowed the costly mink coats of the $100-a-night call girls to wear out in the evenings. One officer, we heard, fell in love with a policeman, and was accused of taking a large sum of money from the inmates' funds on trust here. The head of the institution was reported to have made restitution and then resigned.

The second step after entering was to strip and leave all one's clothes in a side room where they were searched by an officer, while the prisoner was wrapped in a sheet and taken to the showers. Next we were ordered to take an enema and to climb on an examining table for an examination. All openings of the body were roughly searched for narcotics by "a doctor"—a large woman who made insulting remarks about Communists who did not appreciate this country. I told her to mind her business. Once she became so animated in her opinions while she was taking a blood specimen that she allowed the blood to run down my arm. "Watch what you are doing," I said. "Never mind my politics, watch my blood."

Three years later, after the Supreme Court refused to hear our appeal in January 1955, we were rounded up the next day, like fugitive criminals. Ordinarily, the procedure would be to notify the lawyers to surrender their clients in court, at a certain time. Instead marshals came to our homes and we were taken back to jail that afternoon. They could have waited for a few days, as they did not take us to prison until ten days later. Finally, on January 24, 1955, Betty Gannett, Claudia Jones, and I were told to get ready to move. No matter what lay ahead of us, it was a relief to leave the House of Detention. The vile language, the fights, the disgusting lesbian performances, were unbearable. Our only regret was to leave behind three Puerto Rican nationalists. But a few weeks later, when their appeals were denied, they caught up with us in the West Virginia prison.

It was strange to be travelling. For over three years the defendants in our case had not been allowed by court order to leave the Southern Federal District of New York. We were not even allowed to go to Brooklyn, Queens, or Staten Island, which are in another federal district, though part of New York City. We could go up the East side of the Hudson River only as far as the outskirts of Albany. It was a form of house arrest. Once I went into court before Judge Ryan, as a counsel, to ask that the limits be extended to include the beaches in Summer. He looked at me quizzically and said, "Now Miss Flynn, we were both brought up in the Bronx, and you know there are perfectly good beaches there!" So that settled that.

At last, we were now through with the House of Detention. After a sparse meal we gathered up our belongings and were taken to Pennsylvania Station. We were hurried to an employee's locker room on a lower level. It had been sad to see New York City, suddenly grown dear, through the barred windows of a prison van. The U.S. marshal, William Lunney —"the top guy," the others called him—was on hand to see the dangerous Reds off and incidentally to get into the pictures. This he did by walking beside me to the train. Later, after my return from prison, I happened to meet him at Foley Square. I told him I planned to write this book and would mention him. He gave me his card so I'd be sure to spell the name correctly. He's a bit sensitive, too, about how people pronounce it, one of his marshals told me.

Betty, Claudia and I were now en route to a federal prison. It ended one ordeal of four years and commenced another. We had undergone a trial which lasted eight months, a monotonous repetition of the Dennis case. The charge against us was practically identical—"conspiracy to teach and advocate," etc. The government witnesses were the same informers and stool pigeons, posing as experts. The so-called "evidence" was the same, books by Marx, Engels, Lenin, Stalin, and a few American writers. They were trundled into court daily by an FBI agent, in a cart like a baby carriage. Long and unintelligible quotes, torn out of context, were read to a bored and uncomprehending jury. The newspapers lost interest. Spectators dwindled, especially after in a court upstairs, where Senator McCarthy was carrying on his bullying hearings, a man was pointed out by a witness as "a Russian agent," and hauled up as a witness. Many people stayed away from Foley Square.

An appeal to higher courts went on for two years, raising many issues similar to the Dennis case. In rejecting the Dennis appeal, the Supreme Court had refused to review the evidence, the prejudiced method of selecting federal juries, the proven bias of some of the jury, and Judge Medina's conduct of the case. At least the court gave an opinion on the law in that case. But our appeal was rejected without hearings or comment, as was also done in the Baltimore Smith Act case. A few years later, however, the Supreme Court reversed the Smith Act conviction in California. By then a better political climate prevailed and 11 other Smith Act cases around the country and in Hawaii and Puerto Rico were dismissed. We were unlucky to be among the 28 premature Smith Act victims already in prison. The breaks came later. Two of our co-defendants, George Charney and Alexander Trachtenberg, were granted new trials and released from prison, when a paid informer, Harvey Matusow, confessed he had lied in his testimony against them.

The Federal Reformatory for Women is located in a remote Southeastern corner of West Virginia, in a mountainous region. We three women went from New York in two Pullman compartments, made into one. We were accompanied by both a man and woman, federal marshals. They occupied the upper and lower berths on one side, while I occupied the lower and Betty Gannett and Claudia Jones were crowded into the upper, on the other side. There were no curtains between, so I was lying within a few feet of Eddie, the marshal, whom we knew from the courtroom. He was quite embarrassed. He went into the corridor while we undressed. Two other prisoners were in a compartment next door, similarly guarded. One was a young white girl, frightened by the unknown ahead. The other, an older pregnant Negro woman, tried to comfort her.

Before bedtime, we watched the scenery of New Jersey and Pennsylvania fly by the window. We were allowed the luxury of ordering our last meal in what prisoners call "the free world." We treated our fellow prisoners in the next compartment, and the marshals paid the bill, out of our money. Someone had a copy of a slick magazine *Ebony,* which features the achievements and social life of successful prosperous Negroes in the United States. An article entitled "Prison De Luxe" intrigued us. It purported to be a description of the Alderson institution. It emphasized that a few Negro women were employed there as officers. But it said nothing of the difficulties these women had experienced when they first came, of the insults and humiliations suffered from the community and white officers. Neither did it tell of the segregation of Negro inmates and officers which then existed, nor how Negro women were assigned to the hardest, dirtiest, and most menial tasks. We learned all this later. Too bad the editors of *Ebony* could not hear the caustic criticisms of the article by Negro women in the prison, as we did later. But if *Ebony* were to be believed, we were on our way to a mild penal version of a girls' school. We had our doubts, you may be sure, as the train brought us nearer.

[3]

I Become "No. 11710"

We slept very little on the train arriving weary and tense, as do all newcomers to Alderson. It was not yet light. The railroad station was deserted, the little town asleep. There was a covering of snow on the encircling hills. I saw the planet Jupiter, a brilliant morning star, and was cheered by its steady glow. I recalled a line from a song, "The Stars Remain!" We were loaded into a prison bus and driven up a winding road to what looked like a farm gate. A woman officer, shivering in the cold dawn, opened it for us. The marshals were asked to check their guns with her, as none were allowed on "The Reservation." We were driven to a higher level, to a small building with barred windows. This was Cottage 26, then the orientation building. In a dingy room in a rear basement we were greeted by a record officer and filled out entrance forms. Breakfast of coffee and toast was brought to us on trays.

We were next taken in charge by a slender Negro woman officer, whose picture we had seen in *Ebony*. The depersonalizing process began. We knew what to expect, after the House of Detention. We were taken into an examination room and told to strip off all our clothes and deposit them in a bag. The examination was identical, but at least here it was done by a professional nurse without comment. The reason given for this embarrassing search is that narcotics can be and are often secreted in the body. Surely it is not necessary in all cases, where age, past records, etc., are known, especially of political prisoners. But there is no such status in this country, although it is recognized in even the most tyrannical countries.

After a shower we were given rayon nightgowns and brown housecoats of a rough nondescript material, which we saw later in bedspreads, table cloths, napkins, curtains, and dresses. They must have had large quantities of it. Next, "rogue's gallery" pictures were taken, with our numbers in large print across our chests. They were hideously ugly pictures, deliberately made so I believe, so that everyone looks like a hardened criminal. My number was 11710, indicating how many women had passed through this procedure since the prison was opened in 1928. We were fingerprinted, for the third time since our arrest—by the FBI, in the New York jail, and now. Our coats, hats, and suitcases, were stored on shelves to be examined and sorted out later.

For the next three days we were kept in quarantine. Our meals were brought to us and we were taken out only for a daily shower. It was reasonably quiet, though we could hear the scrubbing, waxing, and buffing of floors, which went on continually. A whistle blew to summon the inmates to work in the early morning, to quit at noon for lunch, to return at one, and to quit at five. A whistle blew ten minutes ahead of quitting time. We knew later this was for any men working on the premises to leave before the women came out. Once we heard four blasts of the whistle at night. Later we learned that meant someone had tried "to make bush," prison lingo for escape, and had been caught. There was a dog kennel near the prison. The howling at night was nerve-racking, particularly as we mistakenly thought they were bloodhounds connected with the prison.

My room was at the back of the house, looking out on a little stream known as the Green Briar River, winding beside the railroad tracks. Both disappeared around the curve of the mountains. The meager furniture in these small lock-in rooms was a toilet, wash bowl, narrow bed, a radiator, and a cast-iron small chest with one shelf and two doors. Outside the latter would be called a commode, but for some reason peculiar to Alderson here the toilet seat was politely called "the commode." There were fresh towels, soap, a drinking cup, and two old copies of *Life* magazine, both with articles on Stalin. I wondered if it was accidental that they were left there for me.

A disagreeable experience during this period was to have our hair doused with DDT by an officer who informed us it was for delousing, whether one needed it or not. We were forbidden to wash it out for 48 hours, and the horrible stuff clung for days.

On the day of entry, January 25, 1955, we were handed a slip of paper notifying us of our release date. Mine was April 25, 1957. It seemed a long way in the future, especially as

I automatically added the 30 days I knew I must serve in addition, because of my fine of $6000. Theoretically, this is supposed to be for an investigation of one's assets, although why that could not be done in the twenty-seven intervening months, was one of many government red tape mysteries, especially as we had already agreed to a settlement with the claims department and had commenced paying monthly installments during our appeal period.

The heavy shadow of prison fell upon us in those three days—the locked door and the night patrol. The turning of a key on the outside of the door is a weird sensation to which one never became accustomed. One felt like a trapped animal in a cage. Some women reacted with great emotion, screaming hysterically, demanding to get out, beating on the door with their fists in an excess of fear. To be alone, facing a prison term, especially a long one, was more than they could bear. What bothered me much more, then and all the time I was in prison, was to have the door noisily opened at two AM and a flashlight turned on the room, over the bed, and in my face. It woke me from sleep every night for over two years. Where they expected we might go, with locked doors and barred windows, was another inexplicable prison mystery.

We were asked to submit a list of possible correspondents, to be checked by the FBI, of course. I gave the names of personal friends—Marian Bachrach, Mike Gold, and Richard Boyer all of whom were subsequently rejected. My sister, Kathie, my nephew, and another friend, Muriel Symington, were finally accepted. Later, Professor Robert Morss Lovett of Chicago and Dr. Clemens J. France were accepted. On Dr. Lovett's death, Dr. Alice Hamilton volunteered to write to me and was accepted by my parole officer without a Washington check—so greatly respected was this friend and co-worker of Jane Addams.

During the three days' quarantine I was given an envelope and a piece of paper to write a letter home. It was not easy to sound cheerful. I said to my sister: "This is the hardest time for both of us. But it will pass and become easier with each passing day until milestones come—seasons, holidays, visitors, letters—to make time's passage. Anticipation and foreboding are always harder than reality." But I knew I could not lessen the shock of that number 11710 beside my name. Almost simultaneously with my first letter, Kathie received one from the Acting Warden, requesting information on my past life, activities, and interests. Six pages of forms were enclosed for her to fill out. I have them before me as I write. Needless to say my independent little sister ignored all the questions and replied merely that I could give any information they requested, if I deemed it necessary. Some of the questions were: "Did she get along with her sisters and brothers? Was she obedient as a child? Did she play 'hookey' from school? What kind of work did she do? Did she ever run away from home? Give names of husband, why divorced. Why do you think she became involved in her present trouble? Is she addicted to alcohol or drugs? Age, education, religion, citizenship, occupation, and addresses of all members of her family. What are the plans for her on her return," and so forth, *ad nauseum*.

Such questionnaires went to all prisoners' families. Some were afraid they would lose their visiting and writing privileges if they failed to reply. It was a despicable form of petty spying on a prisoner and her family, and gave the authorities private and personal information about her which they had no right or need to secure. Since there was neither psychiatric treatment nor occupational therapy at Alderson, it was not designed to help the prisoners. Instructions on visiting and correspondence were also sent to the families. Correspondence was limited "Strictly to family and business affairs." Visits were allowed once a month, by a member of one's family or authorized correspondents. The maximum number of correspondents was five, plus attorneys, and all names were cleared or investigated by the FBI before acceptance. Money could be sent in not too large amounts for the prisoners' commissary use; subscriptions to newspapers and magazines were limited to two each, and only from an approved list. No packages or gifts, except candy at Christmas, were permitted. In rare cases of serious illness at home, or a special family anniversary, supervised phone calls were allowed.

The officer in charge of us during the three day isolation period said to me: "Try to rest all you can now. It will be much harder after you enter the orientation period." I tried to follow this advice during my whole prison term. Outside I had been a busy, energetic person. I felt no motivation to be so within prison walls. I decided to take the best possible care of my health, and since I would not reform, and could not rejuvenate, I resolved to make a project of reducing. I was a convict, a prisoner without rights, writing a censored letter. But my head was unbowed. Come what may, *I was a political prisoner* and proud of it, at one with some of the noblest of humanity, who had suffered for conscience's sake. I felt no shame, no humiliation, no consciousness of guilt. To me my number 11710 was a badge of honor.

[4]

Orientation in Cottage 26

After World War II, when many army women became prison officials, military language and ways took over in the women's prison. Guards or wardens of former years now became officers (though they remained cops and screws to the inmates). The top staff had high sounding titles of Captain, Lieutenant, etc. The preparatory period, of three weeks, following military usage, was called "orientation." It preceded classifications and assignment to work by a Board of Administration. It included a medical check-up, shots for typhoid and tetanus, intelligence and aptitude tests. There was a daily reading in orientation of the rules that ostensibly governed the institution. But I discovered later these more often changed without a moment's notice to the inmates or even to some of the cottage officers. Punishment for their violation could be loss of days earned as "good time" or confinement in isolation, or both. In some extreme cases, such as escaping beyond the borders of the reservation, destruction of government property, or passing notes in the visiting room, we were warned that the prisoner could be taken outside to a federal court and receive an additional sentence.

It was a relief to be released on the fourth day from solitary and join other human beings in activities. Betty Gannett and I were together again, but we were disturbed to discover that Claudia Jones had been sent to the hospital on the day of our arrival. She suffered from cardiac asthma and had been in the hospital several times in New York. This had probably influenced Judge Dimock to give her a one-year sentence in contrast to Betty's two years and my three. One day, shortly after we came from isolation, a rumor spread of a death in the hospital due to a heart attack. We were frantic until we heard from Claudia, via "the grapevine," that she was alright. A male prisoner from a nearby institution, doing outside work, was the unfortunate victim.

We were taken in groups to the clinic in the nearby hospital, which was under the jurisdiction of the U.S. Department of Health and Education. There were two women doctors and several trained nurses. The latter is unusual in prisons. Most prisons for men have inmate hospital aides. But many pregnant women came to Alderson, who required professional care. One of the doctors, while weighing me in remarked, "There are no fat people in Russia, why didn't you go there?" (This at a time when Malenkov's picture appeared in the papers!) I replied quietly, "I was sent to Alderson." Betty

Gannett was next in line and was heckled in a similar manner about communism. Next came a woman named Jones. Apparently, the doctor had forgotten that Claudia was not with us. "Oh! Another Smith Act," she said sarcastically. The puzzled woman replied, "No, forgery," to the amusement of all the women present.

We were given lengthy questionnaires to fill out. One question was, "Are you a lesbian?" Some did not know what it meant. One woman had broken her glasses and the question had to be read aloud to her. She answered: "Not now. But from what I've heard of this place, anything can happen here!" Knowing of their heroic struggles to enter the profession, I had always admired women doctors. But in common with all the inmates I heartily disliked the two then stationed at Alderson and we rejoiced when they left shortly afterwards. Their stock answer to complaints by sick women was, "It's all in your mind!" A short time before an amateur play had been given by inmates on a holiday, cleverly illustrating this remark. Silk stockings, cocktails, money, even a baby appeared, as the stage doctor said, "It's all in your mind!"

The medical tests showed I had high blood pressure and arthritis. My knees were stiff and it was painful for me to walk. When I asked for a reducing diet the doctor replied, "Do it yourself," which I subsequently did. In fact, during my entire stay I went to the clinic only to check my blood pressure and weight. The bright spot in the first visit to the clinic was when an inmate aid leaned over while taking a blood specimen and said, "Dorothy sends you her love." The message was from Mrs. Dorothy Rose Blumberg, who was serving a Smith Act sentence of three years, in the Baltimore case. Mrs. Regina Frankfeld had already served a two-year sentence in the same case, and had been released before we came. Mrs. Blumberg was in a cottage on the upper campus, which I passed going to the library on Saturdays. She would come out to greet me, a charming little woman, dressed in blue slacks and jacket, with her hair down her back. She looked like a girl, although she was a grandmother. She was only allowed to walk with me the length of her cottage yard—and we walked at a snail's pace, to snatch these few minutes together and to exchange news of our world outside.

She was loved and respected by all her cottage mates for her kindness and understanding. Shortly before her release, when desegregation occurred, she was transferred to a nearby cottage where Negro inmates had also been transferred. We felt both amused and flattered that Communists were called upon to help integrate prison houses.

The woman who gave me the welcome message was Iva Toguri D'Aquino, who was serving seven to ten years for alleged treason, in wartime broadcasts from Japan. The newspapers called her Tokyo Rose, but it was forbidden to call her that in Alderson. She was released later in a fanfare of publicity and held for deportation. But the proceedings could not be sustained because she was American born, of Japanese origin, which was important in relation to many other deportation cases.

We were taken to the school in the Auditorium Building several times for tests. It is named Willdebrant Hall, after a woman Assistant Attorney General of the 1920's, who sponsored building the prison. I had never taken such tests and I felt like a small boy in Kathie's school who cried because, he said, "I took an examination to be an idiot (for the ungraded class), and failed." I wrote Kathie: "I did very well in general intelligence and verbal aptitude. But you will laugh; I did not do so well in mathematics, or precision observations, suited to engineers, mechanics and artists, according to the text book. My aptitudes, it says, are along the line of writing and public speaking, which is reassuring, after devoting fifty years to them. It would have been quite a shock, at my age, to discover I should have been a carpenter."

At the conclusion of these tests the examining officer, Miss Bowman, told me curtly, "There is nothing here for you!" She was a cold, steely-eyed martinet, who had been an officer in the WAAC's and never let anyone forget it. Later, she became the assistant warden. Betty asked her if there was any organized course in American literature. She replied there was no one here qualified to teach it and remarked, "I only took Lit. 3 myself." So Betty later organized her own course as best she could from the books in the library and passed her list on to others eager to learn. I was in a place where there was nothing for me. But her meaning became clear when another officer, the librarian, said: "We would like to have you and Betty work in the library but it's impossible. Pegler and Winchell would accuse us of coddling Commies!" They seemed most fearful of Walter Winchell, who had attacked the Alderson administration some time before on his radio program, and had made some snide remarks about lesbianism. Inmates were always threatening to see Winchell on their release and "tell all."

No mops were allowed at Alderson. The women were expected to wash and wax the floors of their rooms on their hands and knees. I could not do this. Betty Gannett volunteered to do my floor, as well as her own, and was permitted to do so. I felt badly about this, and I knew she was exhausted and suffered from a heart condition. But waxed floors are more important in Alderson than women, be they old, sick, pregnant, or crippled. A daily inspection was made during orientation for dust on mouldings, windows, doors, radiators, and what not. One exceptionally tall officer about reached the ceiling in her search for a speck of dust. "Bet she doesn't do it at home!" the women would say scornfully.

Smoking in bed and leaving a dirty ash tray were punishable with six o'clock lock-up or loss of smoking privileges. Fear of fire was very great. Fire drills occurred regularly. Extinguishers were on every floor. But what a grim farce this all was when we were locked in at night and every door had to be opened separately by an officer with a key. The cottage officers did not remain at night. Only a few remained on the reservation. Night patrol officers made the rounds at long intervals. On windows without bars there were heavy immovable screens, to prevent escapes. Wax and furniture polish exuded from every cottage. Living rooms were full of upholstered furniture. My one fear in Alderson was of fire at night. It would be a holocaust. Occasionally, a smell of smoke from the dump or the incinerators outside the cottage made me extremely apprehensive.

Most of our time in orientation was spent in repairing, fitting, and sewing the clothing allotted to us. At that time we received either seven cotton dresses or five dresses and three slacks. Later, the number was reduced. Some were old, faded, with unsightly patches. They were to be worn in all seasons— "tissue paper," the women called them in Winter. Women from the South and Puerto Rico suffered severely in cold weather. Socks, low shoes, slips, bras, and rayon panties, completed our wardrobes. Winter coats, rubbers and umbrellas, a scarf and hoods, were also issued. But there was never enough of these accessories and many thefts occurred. There were no gloves or mittens except for some outdoor workers. Betty knitted me a pair of mittens which were stolen from my pocket at the craft shop. These were at a premium.

The clothing had come from army surpluses, and the supply rapidly diminished during our stay. Blue slacks and jackets from the WAAC's, seersucker dresses from the Waves, and long sleeved, well tailored dresses of a deep blue, with large pockets, came from the Coast Guard. By swapping around I finally got two of these and felt real dressed up. The slacks were made for men, usually shapeless, a hideous dark green or khaki colored. Worn with a black jacket, they were virtually a uniform for the masculine-minded partners of the lesbian couples. Slacks were useful of course, for the work crews on the farm, maintenance, and painting crews. In earlier days the women had worn a coverall garment of a feminine cut, which was more suitable and attractive.

In 1955 there were two styles of dresses in many colors; red, green, blue, yellow, brown, and plaids. When I left there was only one style, a coat dress buttoned down the front. The tendency was to uniformity and not to the variety of earlier days. The discarded style had a square neck and short sleeves and was cooler in Summer. They were condemned because the officers said the women turned them down "too low." The women said, "As soon as we like anything in here it is taken away from us!" Variants to the dresses were yellow and white uniforms with caps for nurses' aides; white unforms with caps for food workers; heavy white slacks and jackets for dairy workers, and a dreary shapeless gray apron for laundry workers.

Many garments were too large and had to be taken in with bulky pleats. We were not allowed to cut any of them. Most of the Winter coats were ugly and shapeless, though there were a few well-fitting navy and army coats. I was fortunate that only two dresses of my size were found. So I was measured and five new dresses were made for me in the garment shop, an unheard of event in Alderson. Garments could and should be made new for all. It would be a tremendous morale builder for women, especially for those with long sentences.

We were taught special ways to fold our clothes to fit them neatly in the chests. No hangers were available in any cottage except for the Winter coats, and those were not allowed in the rooms. Another red-tape mystery. We had tests in mending and patching. The officer would cut the work to pieces to prevent another inmate passing it as hers. But we helped each other just the same. Name tapes were sewed in each garment at that time, but before I left this practice was abolished and the names were printed in indelible ink, to prevent stealing.

Adjoining the sewing room was a small laundry with old-fashioned washtubs and boards and two ironing boards with electric irons, a constant source of argument and squabbling. The cottages later worked out schedules giving each woman an allotted time to use them, to prevent violent fights. Some women washed and ironed continuously, as if their lives depended on it. Some, like myself, did as little as possible, and we would allow others to use our time. For to some it seemed to have a therapeutic value. As long as we were allowed to send dresses to the laundry, I took full advantage of it. I reverted to my old IWW teachings of "go slow on the job."

[5]
Orientation Sisters

A special feeling developed for our orientation sisters which lasted throughout our imprisonment. Some were bewildered, frightened, numb, almost in a state of shock. Others were defiant, sullen, angry, resentful, rebellious. Some old timers, called in the language of penology "recidivists," or those who repeat committing crimes and violating parole, were indifferent, or at least putting on an act. They laughed, joked at the fears of others, and wised us up to all the tricks of seasoned inmates. They had contempt for "squares" or non-criminals, people who lived normal lives by conventional standards. Some of our orientation sisters were illiterate, but with native intelligence. Others were childlike, immature, of low-grade mentality, easily led into trouble, especially by men. Tensions were very great at first in a group of strange women from all parts of the country, and very different environments, torn from their families, worried about their children, some with husbands in other prisons—all fearful of the future.

In orientation, many characteristics were exhibited. Petty thievery was common. Racial prejudice was expressed. Negro women from the South were reserved and suspicious, even of other Negro women from the North. One had to win their confidence by deeds not words alone. Some women came from dire poverty and were undernourished. They found comforts even in prison which they never had at home. "You never had it so good!" was a grim prison joke. Others were get-rich-quick confidence women, high spenders, used to all the good things of life. "Came right to Alderson in a Cadillac," was a description that fitted them. Some were hard-working women with toil worn hands; others, with the get-by philosophy, boasted they had never worked. Some were well educated and came from good families, others from broken homes and institutions. They were a cross section of the whole prison population, as I discovered later. No rich women were to be found in Alderson.

None in our group had very long sentences and practically all had been released by the time I left. Many were first offenders and quite young. About half were Negroes, a few were Spanish-speaking. The general prison population showed a large percentage of both. The offenses ranged from theft or forgery of government checks, stealing of cars across state borders, making moonshine liquor or selling liquor without a license, embezzlement, extortion, white slavery or transporting prostitutes across national or state borders, to smuggling, peddling, and using narcotics. It is impossible to tell who is innocent. Many told the most plausible stories, which had already been told to arresting officers, prosecutors, lawyers, judges, juries, and parole officers, until they were letter perfect. Yet the stories might be true. My friend Gus Hall remarked once about going to prison, "You'll find everybody there is innocent—just like you are!" Some few, usually of the underworld, were quite frank in talking about how they "got busted," prison lingo for arrested. They made no bones about their guilt and analyzed their mistakes which led to their arrests. Getting caught was the only real crime in their vocabulary.

Most cases were touching in some way. One older Negro

woman from the South, arrested for passing a bad check, a first offender, impressed Betty and me with her pleasant sensible personality. She had attended Mrs. Mary McCloud Bethune's college in Florida but had not mentioned it in her questionnaire because she did not want to bring disgrace on the school or Mrs. Bethune. One day she was called to the office and told her only daughter had died suddenly. She could go to the funeral if she paid her own fare and that of an accompanying officer. But she had no such amount of money. We all offered to contribute to make up the required amount. But we were told it was not allowed under the prison rules, which discouraged mutual aid. In 1959 when Congressman Celler proposed a bill for annual vacations for qualified federal prisoners, George Meyers, one of the Baltimore Smith Act victims, wrote him a commendatory letter. He suggested two other actions. One was to make federal funds available for semi-annual family visits to prisoners as a vital part of a rehabilitation program. Some prisoners never had a visitor, or received a letter or a dollar from the outside world. Further, he proposed the right of prisoners to attend immediate family funerals, at government expense. He said: "I have seen young teen-agers lie on their bunks and cry their hearts out, with the tears later turning to bitterness. Rehabilitation?"

Among our orientation sisters were two frightened youngsters about sixteen, who were brought in from Texas. Their homes were in New Kensington, Pa. They had taken a joy ride in a "borrowed" car across a dozen state lines with a couple of hometown soldiers, a violation of the Dyer Act which punishes not only the driver but occupants of stolen cars. These were not neglected children, but were indulged by their parents, whom they confidently expected to come at once to take them home. But it wasn't that easy.

They put up a brave front in orientation when they were with the rest of us. But Betty Gannett was assigned to the same dormitory with them because it was discovered that at night they broke down and cried pitifully, like little children. Betty comforted them as best she could. All the women lectured them on behaving themselves. Eventually they were released in the custody of their folks. But it was regrettable how much they had heard of crime, degeneracy, and bad language. Such youthful first offenders should be separated from the boastful loud-talking habitual criminals. The crime committed against them was far greater than what they had done.

There were table cloths and napkins in the dining room. The dishes have the insignias of army, navy, and medical corps. The food was starchy, with noodles, beans, potatoes, and vegetables cooked Southern style in pork fat. Milk was on the table at all meals. There were jellies, jams, cakes, pies, biscuits, and fresh-made bread from the bakery and ice cream every Sunday. You could help yourself plentifully if there was enough to go around, but must eat all you took. Most women passed the food politely. Some gave portions they did not want to a friend. This had advantages for me as many would not eat the occasional grape fruit, tomato juice, spinach, and jello. They were not used to such food and disliked it. Those who had been a long time in jails ate ravenously. Narcotic addicts, many from the Kentucky hospital supposedly "cured," could not get enough food, especially sweets.

There were religious services twice a week and movies once a week, later changed to every other week. Attendance at religious services had once been obligatory, but was now voluntary. Many inmates attended faithfully, some because they felt it would help them to get parole more easily. I did not attend either. I had registered as non-religious and was too tired for movies. I locked in at seven PM during my entire stay there. It was the only period of peace and some degree of quiet. All inmates, from 16 to white-haired grandmothers, are called "girls." We were all addressed by our first names, a disconcerting familiarity at first, but probably just as well, as inmates do not then recall others' full names after release. It reduced chances of blackmail and embarrassment.

Most of the inmates were heavy smokers. Three packages a week were distributed free to each of us. Although I do not smoke I did not so register, on the advice of prison-wise friends. I received my full quota during my entire stay and gave them all away. I estimate Uncle Sam gave me 360 free packages of cigarettes, a small bonus for my time. At first they were Pall Malls and Chesterfields, later an obscure brand of army surplus, heartily detested by the smokers. The only redeeming feature was that these had coupons. At first the officers collected them for their own use. Later, an order came that they were to be saved in each cottage to provide new card tables.

Towards the end of orientation we were taken individually to the basement to check our belongings, to be given what we were allowed to keep and to pack the rest to be sent home, at our expense. I contributed my hat, some surplus scarfs and handkerchiefs for women to have going out. Claudia, Betty, and I had been fortunate to be briefed by a friend who had served a sentence there, as to what we might be allowed to bring in with us. The rules can change of course, with disconcerting suddenness, but we were able to keep quite a few articles, and how precious such ordinary things were! I was allowed two pairs of Red Cross oxford shoes, two pairs of glasses, two sweaters, three pairs of socks, five handkerchiefs, two scarfs, a girdle, comb and brush, a manicure set, toothbrush, toothpaste, talcum powder, a hand mirror, and my son's picture. But I felt outraged that my two brand-new sweaters, with the price tags still on them, were soaked in cold water by an officer and dried out in the storeroom before I could have them. This was another stupid red-tape precaution against narcotics smuggling. It seemed silly when toothpaste and talcum powder were allowed.

Other inmates envied us our possessions and suspected Uncle Sam of playing favorites. They were surprised to learn that they could have brought in similar articles, but nobody had told them. We had verified the information at the House of Detention in New York, but there they did not inform all who were en route to Alderson. It would have been a great help to the women if they could have known in advance what was allowed. It would be simple to have a typed list available at points of detention in time to have friends and families provide the articles. Shoes would be especially valuable. Many inmates suffered from foot ailments caused by prison shoes which were made in other federal prisons. Some were not accustomed to low heels and suffered from "loafers."

There were two bright spots for Betty and me during this period. One was that we discovered a large number of good books in a closet off the living room. This was a godsend as we were not allowed to go as yet to the library or to see a newspaper. Among them was *The Tree of Liberty* by Elizabeth Page, 979 pages, dealing with the American Revolution and subsequently, up to the election of Thomas Jefferson. It was singularly appropriate for us to read in prison; depicting the struggle for the Bill of Rights and Jefferson's repudiation of the Alien and Sedition laws, forerunners of the notorious Smith Act. He had released all the victims and refunded their fines. But we had no Jefferson to complete the parallel for us.

The other bright day for us was when we were called down to the Administration Building, named for Jane Addams, for a lawyer's visit. Since we were not yet allowed out alone, an officer drove us down the hill. Betty, Claudia, and I spent all day with Mrs. Mary Kaufman, our lawyer and friend. To be able to visit with her and with each other, was an unexpected pleasure. We had seen Mary only a few weeks before, but it seemed ages. We were very proud of our "lady lawyer," beautiful, charming, well dressed—"far more stylish than any of the officers," the inmates in the office said later.

Mrs. Kaufman had been one of our trial lawyers and had also been associated with the defense in the Dennis case. She had been an attorney representing the U.S. government at the Nuremberg trials. I could well believe the description given of her role there in cross-examining Nazi war criminals as "devastating." She did a similarly effective job in exposing and discrediting government informers in our trial. She handled my examination as a defense witness for eight weeks, and I was able, under her skillful guidance, to bring in a great deal of explanation as to the true purposes of the Communist Party in contrast to the government's distorted picture. During our imprisonment she participated in the defense in the Smith Act trials in Denver and in St. Louis, and was counsel for Robert Thompson and William Z. Foster. She is a brilliant lawyer.

We met her then and always thereafter in one of the parole officers' rooms. It was supposed to be completely a confidential visit, but we suspected the room was wired for sound. She brought us news of the hearings for a new trial then being held before Judge Dimock, following the Matusow confession. We felt elated. At least the struggle for our release continued and we were not forgotten.

At last came "graduation," which was assignment to our permanent living quarters and to work. It was pathetic to see the women selecting their best dresses, washing, starching and ironing them to perfection; shampooing and setting their hair, trying to look their best. One officer even bought a deodorant for them to use. We walked the length of the upper terrace or "campus" as it was called, down a long flight of stairs, called "the 64's," to the Administration Building to meet "the Big Deal," as the cynical ones dubbed it. We sat on benches outside the parole offices, and were called in one by one. As was evident from the time schedule, it was a cut-and-dried procedure. We were not being consulted, but told decisions already made.

My turn finally came and I was ushered in and motioned to be seated. A group of expressionless women were seated in a semi-circle—parole officers, teachers, other officers, and the warden, Miss Kinzella. I felt their curious stares fixed upon me. There was one man, the Catholic priest. Only the warden, Miss Kinzella, spoke, in a cold, formal, official tone. She warned me of "severe consequences" if I attempted to carry on Communist propaganda while there. She continued that because of my age, weight, and state of health, I had been assigned to live in Davis Hall No. 2 (the second floor) and to do cottage mending. She did not tell me that this place was maximum security, a few steps removed from "solitary" or what they called "seclusion," the punishment area. She did not tell me that among the residents were many misfits who could not live in cottages, some violent and dangerous. Rather, in her smug way, she made it sound as if I were being shown special consideration. She did not tell me that as a political prisoner I would be discriminated against, that I need not expect parole and would get no industrial or meritorious good time off, even if I earned it. All this I learned later for myself.

We returned to orientation quarters, regretfully to bid our new acquaintances goodbye. We felt close to each other and sad to part. I believe it would be a good system to keep such a group together, eliminating only those hard-boiled ones who had a bad influence on the younger. I was the only one sent to Davis Hall. I felt bereft to part with my comrade Betty Gannett, who had been similarly lectured by Miss Kinzella. She was assigned to live on the lower campus and to work in the store-house, a particularly hard job, where she was on her feet all day, carrying and lifting heavy boxes far beyond her strength. Claudia Jones had been delayed by hospitalization and remained in orientation. Later, she was assigned to a segregated "colored cottage" and to work in the craft shop, which was then in the basement of the Auditorium Building. I did not see either of them for many weeks.

On our return to the spacious, nicely furnished first floor of Davis Hall, where we had completed our orientation period, I was told to bundle all my possessions in my housecoat. A barred door was unlocked, I was escorted up a flight of stairs where another barred door was unlocked. I was introduced to a tired-looking officer who said: "I wish I had known you were coming! But we'll do our best!"—cryptic words to me then. I was now a full-fledged prisoner, with a place to live, a job, and commissary and library privileges, with two years and four months ahead of me.

[6]

Maximum Security

Davis Hall is an impressive-looking building, with a stately white pillared front. It is named after a pioneer in prison reform, Dr. Katherine B. Davis, the first woman superintendent of a women's reformatory. Its main floor is attractive and well proportioned. But what a shocking disappointment its second floor turned out to be! The dark hall was long and narrow, with the seclusion punishment cells occupying the full length of each end, shut off behind barred doors and windows. I was ushered into a shabby dilapidated room, with unpainted walls and broken-down furniture. Orientation seemed a fake at this minute! The officer sensed my dismay and said: "Make the best of it tonight. We'll see what we can do in the morning." I put my clothes away in the one workable drawer of the sagging bureau. Not even in a remote mining camp had I stayed in such a room. I put my son's picture on the bureau, but I confess my spirits were low as I went out to the living room that late afternoon.

It was a small room the size of the bedrooms, crowded with nondescript worn furniture, a small center table, and a radio in the corner. It had one window, facing the campus, but it was behind the pillars and we could see little. It was dark and gloomy, with an unshaded hanging electric bulb for light. A couple of women in old slacks, broken-down shoes, no socks, were seated there and greeted me. They certainly did not look like my neat orientation sisters.

The radio blared forth. I had not realized how lucky we had been in Cottage 26 that the radio had been out of order. From then on the radio became one of the most disagreeable features of my prison life. I came to detest it. Invariably, news was shut off for rock and roll, hill-billy ditties, and the juke box review. Girls would run the whole length of the hall screaming: "That's my song!" when a popular favorite was heard. There was so much squabbling over the radio at Davis Hall that finally a night was designated for each inmate to take exclusive charge of the program. I waived my right, although I wished, selfishly, I could silence it for one night, at least. At the end of my term I said to Kathie, "The first thing I want to do at home is to throw the radio out the window." She looked startled and said, "You might kill somebody!"

There was no regular dining room in this strange place. Four or five tables were set up in the hallway. The food came up by dumbwaiter from the kitchen below to a small service pantry. There were about 19 inmates and there was much less formality than in large cottages. Some put their food on trays and ate in their rooms. The sullen, moody ones were humored in this way.

At least half of the women went out to work—to the laundry, garment shop, and craft shop. Others worked in this building in the bakery, kitchen, pantry, on maintainance, or serving the seclusion section. One chatty little lady undertook to enlighten me as to who they all were and why they were here. She described them as attempted suicides, epileptics, lesbians—some she referred to as "studs"—some had maniacal tempers, others were sick and crippled. She did not exaggerate much.

From time to time our number was increased by disciplinary cases just released from seclusion. It was customary to place them in maximum security before they were allowed to return to a regular cottage. Often they were thin and weak from hunger. They felt humiliated, were lonesome for their friends, and would storm and rave. The noise, confusion, screaming, and fighting was sometimes unbearable, both in the cottage part and in the seclusion cells. I felt I was in "a snake pit." I wondered if all of Alderson could be like this. It seemed impossible.

The day after my arrival in Davis Hall No. 2 the officer told me that my new-found friend had offered to give me her room and move down the hall. She claimed she was afraid of a Negro woman across the hall, who had threatened to kill her. Later I knew she had moved to be nearer another inmate she had "a crush on." But I was grateful. It was a larger room with a southern exposure. The walls were painted and she had left a large armchair, two floor rugs, and curtains on the windows. The showers, toilets, and laundry room were a few feet away. At night, when we were locked in, we had a white enamelled covered night jar, which had to be emptied and washed each morning. I was told that for many years the inmates had old-fashioned open-top aluminum chamber pots with handles. They were expected to keep them highly polished. One lifer told me how an officer had complimented her, "You always keep such a nice pot!"

On my first day, a tall thin officer with an Irish name assigned me to clean out the utility closet, where brooms, mops, soap, cans of waste paper, and so on, were kept. It was not hard work and I did not mind it although it hardly seemed to be cottage mending. But after that I only did sewing unless I volunteered for other tasks. The two officers I first met were selected especially for this group and did not rotate as did officers in regular cottages. They were pleasant though firm, and were liked by the women. I worked in my room. There was no other suitable place. I brushed, mended, and sewed buttons on coats to go back to the clothing room. I put the initials "D.H. 2" on new sheets, pillow cases, spreads, mattress covers, towels, wash cloths, and napkins, before they went to

the laundry. I mended all the garments turned in by dis-
charged women who could not sew. It was clean, pleasant
work, and I was not pressured as to speed. I soon began a
voluntary sideline of mending, fitting, and hemming dresses
for inmates, which continued through my entire term and for
which they were very grateful. It added a lot to their appearance.

On Washington's Birthday, 1955, I was given an odd task.
A large number of small brown Bibles (in two-volume sets of
the Old and New Testaments, issued by the U.S. Army during the war, with a message from President Franklin D. Roosevelt) were gathered up. I do not know why they were called
in, possibly because of the change in administration in Washington. Too bad it did not likewise affect J. Edgar Hoover.
I was asked to go through them and clean them up, to erase
all writing. These little worn Bibles were pathetic. They con-
tained names and addresses of soldiers, and of women prisoners, messages addressed home, four-leaved clovers, pressed
flowers, a sprig of lilies of the valley, bits of marked sections
of poetry. But I found nothing vulgar or obscene, written
by either soldiers or women prisoners, though one could find
plenty in library books and magazines. Passages were marked
in the Psalms of David, the Songs of Solomon, and the Ser-
mon on the Mount.

It is not considered good form in prison to ask "what are
you here for?" But as days passed I heard the stories of my
companions. They all were anxious to confide their troubles
at the slightest show of interest. My first friend was lame and
partially paralyzed from an auto accident. She came from the
Midwest, was quite pretty and read a great deal. According
to her story she was a "Bandit Queen" who had organized a
network of robberies, with a crew of youngsters working for
her and "fences" to receive the stolen goods. These included
anything in reach that was movable—wearing apparel, cam-
eras, clocks, typewriters, etc. She boasted of her excellent
memory to be able after her arrest to identify racks of stolen

garments and tell exactly from which store they had come. She had a long sentence in Alderson and "detainers" from several states on her release, which meant further arrests and trials, when her federal sentence expired.

Another of my first acquaintances was an elderly woman from the Pacific Coast called the "Grandma Bandit," who held up a bank with a toy pistol. She was in charge of the records at the garment shop and very competent. She looked as if she belonged in a church rather than in prison. She said she was a Republican and treated me with friendly amusement as the first Communist she had met. Eventually, since she had no criminal record or previous arrests, her friends secured her release on parole. They said it was just "a lark."

Several of my neighbors were drug addicts. They dreamed of the day of release and they longed for a first fix or shot. One worked in our pantry. She was hardworking and kind, but weak-willed and childlike. She suffered pains in her legs and feet, could not wear shoes and at times could hardly stand to work. The veins in her legs were collapsed by perforations of the needle and the doctors could not repair the damage. She would not accept their diagnosis that the habit had brought her to this state. From her conversations it was certain she would return to the old life of prostitution and narcotics. It was like watching a person go to a death sentence, powerless to intervene. Her gentle, "Yes, yes, you are right," meant nothing.

My next door neighbor, from the Southwest, had been arrested for violating the liquor laws, selling whiskey without a license. She would wail, "It was only a pint!" She felt outraged; for a year's sentence it should have been at least a gallon. She was a middle-aged homely woman, but had married a young man and turned over her bank account, car, diamond ring, and finally, her speakeasy place of business. Then her troubles with the law began, undoubtedly at his instigation. He wrote to her in prison a few times. Then she heard no more. A woman friend wrote her that he had sold out and gone to California with a blonde. She attempted suicide by cutting her wrists with a razor blade and landed in maximum security. She worked in the craft shop, the only place with an occupational therapist, who tried to keep her busy. Because I listened to her she made me a leather belt, in gratitude. She left vowing to kill the pair, but we heard no more of her, so guessed she did not find them.

There was no segregation in maximum security. There were three Negro women when I came. One, who was half blind, was assigned to cleaning the hall, the living room, toilet, and wash room. The one who lived across the hall from me worked in the laundry. My self-appointed guide had said on the first day: "She's crazy. Be careful of her." It was evident the little Southerner was full of racial enmity. When the Negro laundry worker came in from work that day, she took off her shoes and rubbed her tired swollen feet with a lotion. She saw me and with a friendly smile said, "Hello." We were good friends until I left. She had worked in a steel plant during the war. She was serving a ten-year sentence for kidnapping a white baby while she was drunk. She had blackened the baby's face, which was naturally very noticeable. She did not recall why she did it, but assured me many times: "I only took the baby for a ride, Elizabeth. I didn't do a thing to hurt her!" She was a hard worker and kept herself and her room immaculate. She was good natured when she felt alright. But suddenly her eyes would cloud up, over some real or fancied grievance, and she would begin to cry and to fight. She was very strong and everyone was afraid of her in these moods. Sometimes I could calm her down and persuade her to give me the chair or scissors she had grabbed as weapons.

One day a girl came running to me. "Quick, Elizabeth," she cried. "A has a scissors down her dress and wants to kill M." I went to the living room and sat down beside my friend. I asked her what was wrong. She began to cry and tell me her grievance against a trouble-maker who sat in another chair, afraid to move, frozen with fear. I said, "Give me the scissors. You will be in trouble." She gave them to me. Then I told the other woman to leave. She scurried away. I gave the scissors to a friendly officer who returned them where they belonged without reporting it.

About three weeks later, A came to me troubled. "Elizabeth, what did you do with the scissors?" she asked. I reassured her all was well, she had nothing to fear—to her great relief. It saved her from seclusion or worse.

Once when she was in seclusion, I borrowed all the fruit and candy she had in her room for a farewell party for one of her friends. I left an IOU in her basket. At first when she saw the fruit gone, she was very excited. But the IOU signed by me amused her greatly. She said, "It's as good as money any day."

She was very proud of my friendship and would say in explaining why she heeded my advice, "Elizabeth is just like a mother to me." The women doctors did nothing to help her. But later when two young men doctors came, they took an interest in her and gave her medicine to quiet her before her monthly periods. She became much better. I hated to leave her there and wondered what would happen to her outside. My most vivid recollection of her was when she was placed on a holiday musical program by an understanding officer. She was very proud and practiced diligently. She wore a nice long white dress from the costumes used for plays. She sang "In The Chapel" in a pleasant voice. How much could have been done with kindness and understanding for women like her. But few cared or realized this. "Crazy" was the prison verdict on her.

In this forlorn group was a beautiful Spanish-speaking woman, accused of "white slavery" or transporting Mexican women over the border to Southwestern houses of prostitution. She danced to the radio, sang gay little songs, spent all her spare time in the craft shop, where she made beautiful purses and belts of fine design and tooling. Poverty, drugs, men—this was her story, like so many others there. It seemed incredible that such a nice young creature could be so evil. Isolated from her abhorrent trade, sitting opposite me, passing the sugar, I thought as I looked at her and others around me, what a waste of human material; what she and they might have been, under a different social system! No attempt is made in prison to salvage them.

[7]
Seclusion

Years ago, when this institution was established, "seclusion" had an entirely different meaning. It was actually solitary confinement, and was then considered a last resort, when all other attempts at correction failed. It was used only for the most serious offenses. Now it was resorted to for all kinds of petty infractions as well, at the whim of officers. In men's prisons "solitary" usually referred to what was called "the hole" or dark, underground cells. Here, at least, it was on the second floor, where there was light and air and the victims could see and talk to passers-by. They were forbidden to do so, but they did. These cells at the end of our corridors were usually full of screaming, shouting women, who fought with each other through the windows. Day and night till lock-up time inmates would risk a disciplinary, to deliberately walk that way to console an imprisoned friend. The favorite Alderson salutation was: "I love you! I miss you! Do you hear?"

Sometimes the lock-ins hammered on the doors for hours at a time, screaming to get out. One day a girl in seclusion set fire to the mattress. How she had concealed matches was a matter of intimate discussion. When the guards came to put the fire out, the girl had hysterics. After that for a while mattresses were taken out. We saw the unfortunate seclusionists when they were brought in or taken out to our corridor for showers, dressed only in a nightgown and housecoat. Women charged that the guards were rough in handling them, pushing them along and hurling them into the cells.

The most serious violation of rules was to attempt to escape. Many attempts had been made, but they quickly ended within a few hours with the escapees being caught. They were never the well-planned organized group efforts that occur in men's prisons, and were easily handled. They were usually on the impulse of the moment by rash youngsters. To "make bush" was rarely attempted by older women or those who are prison-wise. There were no walls around the reservation, but the people in the area are alerted to help capture an escapee and collect a $50 reward. "That's a lot of money to the yokels around here," the women would say. The local people were fearful too of being arrested on a harboring charge, a federal offense, if they helped an inmate in any way. Some such prosecutions had occurred and deterred the natives from being kind-hearted. One man picked up two girls in his car and drove them right back to the prison before they could protest.

City-bred inmates were afraid of the mountain country and the presence of snakes, skunks, and wild animals, and would not venture beyond the reservation and the roads leading to it. Anyone who attempted escape would lose many days, sometimes all their statutory time. Those who managed to get outside the reservation were charged with further violations, especially if a window or lock was broken or a screen cut. Yet the urge to freedom was so great that women have broken arms and legs jumping from second-story windows. Desperate youngsters would try over and over again. Two kids hid in a coal car standing on the tracks near the prison where a search revealed them. They were a sorry sight, covered with coal dust, as they were marched to seclusion. Another was fished out of the little stream bordering the reservation.

One day a big hue and cry was raised because an officer looking out of a window saw a girl in brown slacks walking along the tracks. A count was made of the entire prison population, but no one was missing. The local police were notified and discovered that a town woman had taken a short cut on an errand. The officers were chagrined, but the inmates got a big kick out of the incident. If there ever has been any successful escape from Alderson it was kept hush-hush. One Indian girl who was not afraid of wild country was rumored to have made it. Another rumor told of a woman who made herself a nun's habit, had friends waiting just outside, and got away safely out of the country. A woman was brought back from Washington, D.C., while I was there, who had worked for quite a while in a supermarket, before an eagle-eyed sleuth discovered her.

One day two youngsters walked out of our cottage ostensibly to go to work and pulled a fake escape. They hid in a tree, directly in back of Cottage 26. All the officers who were off duty were called back on such occasions. The entire area was alerted. The woman who worked in the photograph room was advised to make up a number of pictures of the two missing ones for the FBI, state and city police, and sheriffs. The guards and officers searched every cottage, looked under the beds, overturned the haystacks on the lawns. The railroad cars on the sidings were all searched. A guard climbed to the top of the water tank to survey the countryside. They beat all the bushes. It was sickening to behold, a regular manhunt. Finally, an officer spied them perched in the tree. The two weary and hungry escapees climbed down, begged for a cigarette, and were taken to seclusion in the Warden's car. There was great hilarity among the inmates, and anger among the hot and tired guards.

Some inmates were in and out of seclusion every few days. One such lived with us in Davis Hall. The first time I saw her she was doing a tap dance to the radio, a little white sailor cap on her blonde curls. She looked like a teen-ager, but I was amazed to hear she had been married twice and had three children. Two had already been adopted through the Welfare Department in her home city. From her earliest youth she had been in institutions. She had the reputation of being the wildest, most unpredictable, and incorrigible inmate in Alderson. She had been in practically every cottage on the reservation. The first morning I was there she refused to do her work, refused to go to her room, and was finally put in seclusion. Another day she suddenly smashed everything breakable in her room.

A few days after that she and another juvenile, an Irish-American girl from Coney Island, tore up sheets and spreads in her room, tied them together a lá movie scenes, and tried to drop out a front window to a broad street below with people and cars going back and forth continuously. For this silly prank, like boarding school kids, they both went to seclusion.

Fighting was the second most serious offense. No matter what the circumstances both contestants were sent to seclusion, which was certainly not fair, as often one was the aggressor and the other the victim. But no attempt was made to investigate and fix the blame. An inmate could easily be framed in this manner. Razor blades were sometimes used in deadly manner in fights. Held flat between two fingers, they were a deadly weapon. I mended a pair of slacks for an inmate with a wicked cut six inches long from a blade wielded in a fight. She had a scar on her leg. Another girl was cut on the eyelid, narrowly escaping serious eye injury. In another case a young girl was stabbed by a jealous older woman. A knife, stolen from the paint crew and sharpened like a stilleto, barely missed her heart. Many of these battles were between jealous lesbian couples.

Try as they would the officers had a hard time keeping track of razor blades. They were allowed to inmates to cut corns or for cleaning paint spots from windows. Often the inmate "forgot" to return the blade, officers went off shifts, replacements took over on their day off, and the blades were forgotten in the shuffle. They were well hidden, in the seams of the curtains, for instance. Finally, inmates were only allowed to use them in the presence of the officer, to reduce the hazard. One girl came to me in tears, asking for advice. She worked in the kitchen and handled knives, large and small. She said her father had been a knife thrower in a circus and had taught her all kinds of tricks with knives. But she was very high-tempered and was afraid of what she might do. She wanted to be taken out of the kitchen away from the knives and given work free of this danger. I talked to one of the officers who referred her to her parole officer and she was transferred to farm work.

Another extremely prevalent offense which led to seclusion was to be "caught in the act" of a lesbian affair. Short of being so caught the practice was accepted and ignored. Of course it was not easy for officers to keep track of all these attachments and performances. Many tricks were used to evade scrutiny. One girl would sometimes keep the officer busy at her desk with some legitimate request, while her friends "played" upstairs. A friend would stand watch, to sing or whistle if the officers started upstairs. This was called "jiggering." An inmate who habitually whistled was in hot water all the time with both inmates and officers. When caught in the act or in a violent quarrel, the pair were assigned to separate cottages, after a term in seclusion. At first they were lonely and unhappy, sending illegal messages or "kites" to each other. But out of sight, out of mind, was the usual rule and they soon forgot each other and took up with somebody else.

Many accusations were made by the women who had been in seclusion, the truth of which I cannot vouch for as I was never there. Officers and guards were not allowed to use violence at any time, but the women charged them with it.

They charged that the regular night jars were taken out of the seclusion cells and the women given paper cups in which to urinate at night. One woman was reported to have thrown the contents in the face of an officer. It was said Mr. James V. Bennett, director of the Bureau of Prisons, ordered the mattresses replaced, after a visit there. Seclusion seemed about as effective as putting a child in a dark closet. If it were used rarely as Dr. Harris did earlier, to merely allow an inmate to regain her composure, it might help. But as it was, the victim became bitter, sullen, and smarting with a sense of injustice, especially for trivial offenses. The loss of statutory days was a much more serious punishment in the graver offenses, than seclusion.

[8]
Prison "Privileges"

One was constantly reminded in prison that you had no rights, only privileges which could be snatched away without explanation. Anything you were allowed to have or do was a privilege. Commissary was such—for those who had the money to pay for it. At that time a store was set up in a small room of Cottage 27, which was a twin of 26, and was originally intended for mental cases. Some officers had quarters on the second floor. They might as well be inmates, living behind barred windows. The commissary office was a distance from there, in the Administration Building—another example of prison inefficiency. Every Saturday, commissary day, articles were lugged in a car from the office to the store. The commissary officers had inmate assistants but they were changed often, to avoid thefts. The store was too small, and women crowded in, a few at a time. Others hung around in the hall, waiting their turn, but they enjoyed this chance to chat with friends from other cottages.

One or two cottages were called at a time. At first everybody went Saturday. Later, it was changed to alternate Saturdays for each campus, to avoid the overcrowding and fraternization. There was an upper and a lower campus day. The commissary officer had a file of cards with the inmate's name, number, a picture, and the amount of money received and spent. At first $13 a month was allowed for commissary. Later, in deference to increased prices, it was raised to $15. If you did not use the full amount the balance did not go over to your next month's commissary, but remained in your funds. However, extra amounts, not chargeable to your commissary, could be drawn from your funds for newspaper subscriptions, book orders, craft shop supplies, material for the dressmaking classes, and the like. We Communist women were most fortunate in that we always had funds on hand. Many others were penniless or received only an occasional dollar or two from home. You could not give another inmate money and you were forbidden to buy commissary for others. This rule was usually winked at, though it could be invoked suddenly. However, it was violated continually by all of us. In stock were candies, cigarettes, fruit, cookies, crackers, kleenex, also cosmetics which included soap, face and talcum powder, lipstick, deodorants, cold creams, shampoos, and hair oils. Fruit meant oranges, lemons, and apples. Prices were as high as in an outside store, and sometimes higher. Brands were limited to one or two. One wondered how it happened that one company was favored over another. One would be naive to believe it accidental, but of this suspected graft in prison I was never in a position to ascertain facts.

My needs were simple, but I spent all my allowance. Like my comrades, I gave away much of what I purchased. I had a list prepared in advance from requests from my cottage sisters. My little blonde neighbor was very proud and would ask for nothing, though she did not have a cent. It was hard to persuade her to accept a candy bar or a piece of soap, which was unusual in a place full of "moochers." I gave her my large box of talcum powder. "From the free world," she exclaimed delightedly. Then she said very seriously: "I steal, Elizabeth. But I'll never steal from you. And I won't let anybody else do it either!" She stood guard and challenged everyone who tried to enter my room, if I was absent. Woe betide anyone who tried to steal from me after that!

Inmates were allowed to place articles on sale which they had made, such as metal and ceramic jewelry, pins and earrings, pottery and ash trays, vases, knitted sweaters, scarfs, mittens, infants' wear, and woven articles such as place mats, center pieces, tea towels. Articles made by inmates could be exhibited in glass cases in the Administration Building and the visitors' room. The materials were purchased at the inmate's expense and the articles made on their own time. Prices were fixed by a committee of officers from the commissary and craft departments. Occasionally, in a destitute case, materials were advanced to give the inmate a start.

During my stay in Alderson I bought a great deal of ceramic jewelry to give to friends on my release. I also arranged with my sister Kathie to buy several beautiful stoles in the visitors' case, at $10 each. This we did to help the Puerto Rican nationalist women, who had crocheted them. They arranged with the craft shop officer to put them on the shelves the day Kathie came. Officers could also buy articles and order special things from inmates. They got beautiful articles at low cost, far less than they would pay outside. The funds were a great help to those who had no other source of income. It was rumored that some orders originated in Washington and were for government people, who had seen the quality of the goods while visiting Alderson.

Another "privilege" was to visit the library for one hour, on Saturday. Later the librarian extended my period to two hours. It was a walk of about three blocks from the cottage.

The library was the most pleasant and attractive place in the prison. It consisted of two large book-lined rooms, with comfortable chairs, nice plants and ferns, pictures on the walls and several busts of children. There was a large assortment of books, many of which came from nearby army Camp Croft, when it was disbanded. These of course were dated, up to 1945. There were many classics, biographies, standard fiction, and poetry, but few of recent publication. There were some current magazines and newspapers. Among the books were quite a few by progressive authors. But I was careful not to mention or praise such books, lest they be removed as subversive. A library helper told me that they had been instructed at one time to remove all books by certain authors. But with the perversity that abides in prisons, and with no knowledge of the contents, they just shifted them around to other shelves. Fortunately, the arrangement of books was chaotic.

Inmates could also buy books, two at a time. But what a complicated, maddening procedure it turned out to be. The choice had to be cleared with the Warden, the books came directly from the publisher and they had to be read by the librarian before the inmate finally received them. It was a frustrating ordeal. But I did manage to get a few—Sean O'Casey's plays, *The Thomas Mann Reader, The Almanac of Liberty* and *Russian Journey,* the last two by Supreme Court Justice Douglas. I doubt if these would have been acceptable except for the author. At the request of some of the women I also secured Walt Whitman's poems and *The Nun's Story* by Kathryn Hulme. I received as gifts from the outside, a Bible and a dictionary. Dr. B. Liber, an old friend, sent me his autobiography, but it was returned as "unsuitable." In it he had written of his country of birth, now Socialist Rumania. John Abt, one of our lawyers, sent me *The Mandarins* by Simone de Beauvoir, a best seller that year, but it was rejected as "too political." Some of the women were disappointed, as they had heard it was also real "sexy."

Books purchased had to be donated to the prison library as soon as they were read and before others could be ordered. The reader will be amused to know that one of the books now on the shelves in the Alderson federal prison, purchased by this well-known Communist leader, is *Profiles in Courage,* by Senator John F. Kennedy, now president of the United States. I was attracted to it in reading reviews, because it had a chapter on Governor John Altgeld of Illinois, who sacrificed his political career when he pardoned the imprisoned anarchist labor leaders of the 1886 strike for eight hours. It would be admirable if the author would follow this historic precedent and free Morton Sobell and other political and labor prisoners of 1962.

Betty Gannett contributed to the prison library two volumes of Theodore Dreiser, which she had quite a struggle to secure. There were doubts as to the suitability of this great American writer. I made a suggestion to the librarian that many publishers and writers, particularly women, would gladly donate books to the prison library. It was curtly rejected, as usual with any suggestions from an inmate, although later officers would often come up with them as their own ideas and get credit for them. The officer answered me, "We are not allowed to receive donations." This was not true. All the pictures had been donated. Autographed books from well-known personalities were on special shelves. All our unexpired newspapers and magazine subscriptions, were taken over by the library. And they certainly accepted our books, which were involuntary gifts.

A large number of inmates came to the library, not all to read, of course. It was a rendezvous as well, as was church, music appreciation, the craft shop, the movies, and what have you. Many were steady readers, some of excellent books. Some read only mystery stories, of which there was a large supply. Poetry, too, was a favorite, especially about love. Some searched for books with salacious passages and found them. There was a juicy book called *The Widow,* which made the rounds of the cottages surreptitiously, but was not returned to the library for fear it would be taken out of circulation. Proust became a sudden favorite when some one accidentally discovered some of his themes. I was surprised at how little youngsters just out of school read, in contrast to some of the older women who struggled to master words and understand what they read.

We were permitted to subscribe to one daily paper and one magazine. I chose the *New York Herald-Tribune,* and the *Nation,* and Betty Gannett got *The New York Times* and *World News and Review.* A former political prisoner, Mrs. Frankfeld, had insisted on getting the *Nation,* arguing that her husband got it in Atlanta Penitentiary. So, thanks to her, we read it. We were allowed to exchange our periodicals with each other through the prison mail bag, but nothing could be written on them. Written messages (or "kites", as they were called) between inmates, were forbidden and punishable by seclusion, a senseless rule which was violated by all of us. The only rules I respected were the ones that were for the safety or good and welfare of all.

A bundle of the *Christian Science Monitor* came to the library from Charleston and remained unopened. After I had been there a long time and the librarian had become acquainted with me, she would give me the bundle to take to my cottage. It was a good paper, with news of the whole wide world and I appreciated it. But I had to smile at giving a "subversive" an uncensored package from the outside world. The first day I went down to the Administration Building to sign for my newspaper, was unforgettable. It was one month to the day since I came to Alderson and I had never been out of doors *alone.* A fog came right up to the windows. It had frozen on the trees into a beautiful silver, etching every branch. Later the sun broke through and I walked slowly in sunshine to prolong my first few minutes of freedom.

But I must explain what "alone" meant. The commissary

office had called the central control desk and asked for me. "Control" called my cottage. When I left commissary to return I had to report to the central desk. On arrival at my cottage, the office called "Control" to report. Wherever you were "Big Sister" was watching you. They had a roll call before breakfast and at work, on arrival. Absentees were reported to "Control," who checked whether they were ill and locked in their rooms, at the hospital, in seclusion, or with a visitor. There were checks in the cottage at noon and evening meals and in the middle of the night. "Control" knew where every inmate was at all times. Protective custody and detention were no idle words.

[9]

Visitors and Letters

Another blessed privilege were visits from the outside world which were allowed once a month. I had urged Kathie not to attempt to come until the weather moderated, much as I longed to see her. One afternoon in early March the officer said, "Elizabeth you have a visitor." I was so excited I did not change my clothes, although I now had my new dresses, rayon stockings and girdle available. I rushed down as I was—socks and all—to the lower campus, not to lose a minute. The visitor's room is in a cottage near the main office. It is large and sunny, looking out on the lawn and beautiful trees of the lower campus. The furniture is comfortable, arm chairs and settees, to impress the visitors. There was Kathie, with a new dress, a fancy hair do, and a spiffy ittle hat. I was so surprised and delighted I could hardly speak. She was full of news. I was glad she had acted on her own initiative. The strain was acute for both of us and it was well to get it over. The first visit was the hardest.

The institution does not look like a prison from the outside, rather more like a hospital or school. The green lawns and trees, the many cottages and the absence of bars, at least where visitors might see them, makes it less forbidding. Many inmates told their visiting small children it is a hospital. The inmates and their visitors sit in separate family groups around the room, with one or two eagle-eyed and sharp-eared officers constantly surveying the scene. They sat us right next to the officer's desk at first, but later relaxed this vigilance a little. Betty Gannett and her husband were annoyed excessively and complained about the officers sitting practically between them.

Kathie was a master of guarded double-meaning conversation. When the officer was busy at the 'phone or took someone to the toilet in the cottage, she rapidly told me news of other prisoners, and cases and of my dear friends. Then she relapsed back into neighborhood gossip or family matters. The visit was from one to four in the afternoon. Later, Kathie arranged to come every two months for two days—the last day of one month and the first day of the next month, thus taking the allotted visiting days for both months together. It was much less wearing on her and cut the expense in half. It was an ordeal but she came faithfully in all seasons.

Her fares, plus our expenses for commissary, books, subscriptions, etc., were paid for by the "Families' Committee of Smith Act Victims," consisting of wives and families of all who were arrested under this law. Mrs. Peggy Dennis was chairman of this committee. These devoted women not only raised sufficient funds for all Smith Act prisoners, but also enough to send their young children to summer camps and to provide for emergency needs of families. Each one had personal problems, but they made speeches, arranged affairs, wrote articles, for this labor of love. We were envied by less fortunate women (as I am sure our men comrades were in

Atlanta, Leavenworth, and elsewhere by their fellow prisoners), who were greatly impressed by our accounts of this committee's activities. "Communists must be good people!" one
girl said wistfully. She never received as much as a postal card
from outside. Betty Gannett's family came regularly, as did
Claudia Jones' father, who was elderly and not too well. He
had to seek out a boarding house in Alderson, where families
of Negro inmates were welcome. There was a mean atmosphere in this town that lived on the prison.

Kathie fared but little better. At first she stayed in a boarding house near the station, recommended by the deputies
from New York. But apparently, while they welcomed deputies and officers as guests, relatives of prisoners were treated
rudely and discouraged from coming there. Kathie found a
hotel, a miserable dirty place, which once caught fire while
she was there. It was right next to the railroad and trains rat-
tled back and forth all night. There was no key to the door
and Kathie felt certain all her reading matter had been
searched while she was at the prison. I wouldn't be surprised
if it had not been done by the FBI. They must have been
amazed to find a history of art, which she was studying. The
food at this place was typical of the poor South, heavy, taste-
less, and swimming in grease. A taxi drove the visitors to the
gate of the prison, where they were picked up by a guard with
a prison car. They had to arrange for the taxi to call for them
later.

At the end of visiting time, parting was no "sweet sorrow,"
but one of tears, hysterics, and grief. Some visitors came from
far away and might not be able to come again. Husbands and
wives clung to each other and children cried desolately, as
they left their mothers. Old parents were the saddest sight,
trying to smile and wondering, I presume, how it all happened to their dear one. Kathie and I felt bad to part but we
knew it was only for a few weeks and each knew the strength
of the other. She tried to comfort the departing ones on the
way back and I tried to cheer up my tearful companions. We

had to wait in the visiting room till word was telephoned that all visitors were off the reservation, a meaningless rule, like so many there.

Another "privilege" was to write and receive letters. We were allowed to write three a week. The stationery was given out. What was not used had to be returned. For the first few months I wrote them all to Kathie until others were cleared. We could write to our lawyers, if necessary. It was not easy to write these letters, especially at first, to be cheerful, but not to create any illusions about the place. Outgoing letters were read first by the cottage officer, added to her many petty chores. She turned them back if there was any bad language, abuse or remarks about other inmates. One could only write of the place in the most general terms, preferably uncritically. The letters we politicals wrote were also read by our parole officers, as was our incoming mail. This slowed down the process of sending and receiving letters. I believe copies of some, if not all, went to Washington. It is surprising how one can learn to say a great deal, although it may not always be clear to the recipient. But I told Kathie not to mind, I wanted to be able to refresh my memory later, which I have been able to do from my letters. I was not allowed when I left to take my incoming mail home, except for a few letters, so I destroyed them after I replied.

I regretted exceedingly not being allowed to keep the wonderful letters I had received, especially from Muriel Symington. She wrote faithfully several times a week—very witty and informative letters dealing with world politics, campaigns, the amnesty movement, people, events. She copied whole editorials from papers I did not receive, such as the *New York Post*. She sent me beautiful picture post-cards; scenes of New York City, cats, bridges, anything I asked her to find for me. Two replicas of stained glass windows from the cathedral at Chartres and Nòtre Dame were lovely Christmas greetings. One officer who read my letters remarked: "Your friend, Miss Symington, is a most interesting writer. I enjoy all her letters. She must be very well informed." Her clever references to the authorities there and in Washington amused me greatly. I am eternally grateful to all my correspondents who brought the outside world so graphically to me, but especially to Muriel Symington.

I received no cards or letters from anyone but my accepted correspondents. Hundreds arrived for all three of us. Officers told us the mails were clogged on one holiday by our cards. Not only were they not delivered to us while there, but they were refused to us when we left. I regret that our lawyers were so busy that I could not persuade them to start a suit. The excuse given to us at Alderson was, "Now they are government property." A prisoner did sign permission to open and censor her mail, but she did not sign permission to confiscate it. It is a neat legal question: Does the Department of Justice have the right to confiscate U.S. mail? What disposition was made of our letters? They were not returned to the senders. Many did not have return addresses. I have no doubt the FBI had a look at all of them. A personal friend from days prior to my joining the Communist Party, the widow of a U.S. Army major, wrote me a sympathetic letter, which I never saw, of course. Later she was visited by the FBI who asked this surprised lady, "What Communists do you know?" Her letter was the only possible explanation for the visit. I felt, and still feel very indignant at what I considered the outrageous theft of my mail by the U.S. Government.

I encouraged my correspondents to send me a lot of holiday greeting cards, picture postal cards and the like, once I knew it was permissible. I urged them to write their return address, required by prison regulations, in pencil, so I could erase them before I gave them away. This was necessary to protect my correspondents from begging letters or unwelcome visits from released prisoners. I gave the cards out freely and they travelled all over the reservation to decorate rooms. We were not allowed to use thumbtacks or scotch tape, so had to devise ways to fix the cards in the moldings with paper waddings.

Necessity is certainly the mother of ingenious inventions in prison.

Reading over my letters I realize I tried to make the best of everything. "Sufficient for the day is the evil thereof," was my motto. There are two ways, it is said, to do a prison term. One is to beat your head against the wall and the other is to "play it cool." Actually, one did both, as conditions differed. The reader should understand that this special showcase prison was better than state or county institutions, and undoubtedly much better than the older prisons for men, which were built on the cell block system, with as many as eight men in a cell in Atlanta. All the time I was in Alderson, I had a room to myself. I could lock in my room at seven o'clock in preference to going to the general living room, and read or write until nine, when the lights went out. No one resented this, probably on account of my age.

Fortunately, I did not play cards, so was not in demand for that. Possibly they felt relieved because my presence apparently inhibited many from discussing topics of interest to them, in their accustomed four-letter language. I was treated courteously by all but a few. No bad language was ever addressed to me and little spoken in my presence. I have heard some one say, "Hold it, Elizabeth is coming!" before resuming their picturesque lingo. But like all other inmates I hated the place and resented every minute "with a purple passion," as the girls used to say. I never met a woman there who did not share this feeling. One counted the months, the weeks, the days, until release. "Stone walls do not a prison make or iron bars a cage!" But prison is prison, as Alderson proves, even if there are no walls and few bars.

"What Did You Do?"

The most pleasant feature of Alderson was nature's work, the beautiful countryside and the changes of seasons. By St. Patrick's Day spring was in the air. Daffodils, jonquils, and tulips appeared. Blackbirds and robins came, advance agents of Summer. A mother skunk came to Davis Hall kitchen to be fed, leading four babies in a row. Skunks regularly raided the garbage cans at night, scratching the lids off and crying like cats, if they failed. Cats and dogs were *persona non grata* with Miss Kinzella, although in former years, before her time there, they were allowed on the grounds and many officers had pets. But in spite of harsh orders, inmates fed and cared for those that appeared, taking care of mother cats and kittens and lavishing affection on stray dogs. An officer who gave me a lift down the hill on a cold day had her dog in the car. As she slowed down to let me out she said to him, "Get down, you know you're contraband," and he hid under the seat. Even dogs learn to deceive to outwit stupid prison rules.

The younger ones felt sorry for me, a shut-in in the cottage these Spring days, and would bring me little bouquets of flowers, though it was strictly forbidden to pick them. By this time both inmates and officers were curious as to why I was in maximum security and would ask, "Elizabeth, what are you in for?" It was not easy to explain. If I said, "Under the Smith Act," it mean nothing to them. They knew the Dyer Act, the Mann Act, the Harrison Act, the Boggs Act, but Smith—who was he? If I attempted to explain the ideological connotations of thought-control they did not understand. They would insist, *"But what did you do?"* That was even harder to answer. I had not even been accused of writing a specific article or making a particular speech. After all, one is supposed to be accused of doing something to land in prison —steal a car, rob a bank, forge a check, peddle dope, make moonshine, extort money, or commit a murder. What could I say?

Finally I would say, "Well, you see, I'm a Communist." A light broke over their faces. "Why didn't you say so. Now I understand," they would say. But lest they misunderstood and thought I meant to be a Communist is a criminal thing, I explained further about our trial and our closing statements made to Judge Dimock. I quoted a few words from mine as follows:

"Time was when the Communists alone raised slogans for peace, for security, for jobs, for democracy, for unionism— which are on the minds and lips of millions of Americans today. Our lives, our work, our aspirations are part of the American scene for the past half century. Our predecessors go back a century or more. Somewhere and soon the Smith Act will go into the discard as did the Alien and Sedition laws of 1800, the Fugitive Slave laws of the 60's, the criminal syndicalist laws of the 1920's." They stood around wide-eyed and one said, "Gee, that was telling them!"

To be sure they understood, I said I also asked the Judge this question: "If the Communist Party is not illegal, its membership and officership is not illegal, if advocating Socialism is not illegal, if advocating a day-to-day program of 'good deeds,' as the Government cynically calls it, is not illegal, what in all conscience is illegal here? Of what are we guilty?" They nodded their heads.

One girl got quite excited. "Haven't you got a right to your politics under the Constitution?" she demanded. "Well, I thought I did," I replied, "but here I am." Indignantly she burst out: "Why you've got as much right to be a Communist. . . ." She groped for a comparison, and finally ended,

"As I have to use marihuana!" Everybody roared laughing, as this well-intentioned remark floored me.

I had only two unpleasant experiences with inmates because of my views. Of one, with a stool pigeon, I'll write later. The other was an old lady I met one cold day on the library steps. "It's very cold," I said. She glared at me and growled, "It's colder in Russia!" I replied, "Really? I've never been there yet." One of my friends said, "What's eating her? You spoke to her politely." I explained, "She probably thinks all Communists are Russians." My friend retorted: "The old fool! Well, anyhow, she's leaving soon!" They were happy to see people go out whom they liked, but even more glad to be rid of the disagreeable ones. Thus all were speeded on their way, either with kisses or with curses.

I almost learned to tell time at night by the coal cars passing, whose lights flashed in my window. Once I counted 104 cars in one train. They reminded me of the coal miners of West Virginia, who daily risked their lives in the deep dangerous recesses of the earth. Many terrible disasters have occurred in this area. I recalled many trips around this beautiful state, when I had spoken in union halls to the miners. How they must have despised John Lautner, who, as Communist state organizer before the war, had arranged these trips and who had later testified in Smith Act trials as a government informer. He had acted as chairman, sold the literature, taken up the collections, at all my meetings and then lied as to our purpose there. I knew there were many coal miners who would gladly have testified for me and refuted his version of my speeches. But I could not ask them to do that. They would have lost their jobs and homes and been forced to leave what were virtually company towns. But I knew that many of them remembered me and were indignant that I was back now in their state, in a prison. This comforted me.

There were no correspondence courses available at Alderson while we were there. Betty Gannett who was more ambitious than I and is a born teacher, secured data on college courses in English from one of the volunteer religious workers. She passed the information on to others who were interested and helped cottage mates to learn to read and write. A large number of the Negro women from the South and some from elsewhere were illiterate, as were many of the older white women. I felt sorry for women who could not read. It was a great solace in prison. Classes were held at the school to teach reading and writing. Attendance was obligatory for all inmates of school age and there was a large number. High school classes were also available and diplomas from the State of West Virginia did not show that they were earned at Alderson. However, there were not enough qualified teachers and none volunteered from the community. Inmates with better education were assigned to teach classes but often were ill prepared, unwilling, and indifferent. Betty Gannett could have made a real contribution. But they were fearful that even the ABC's could be Communist propaganda. In all the cottages friends helped each other. It was a hit or miss system, like everything there.

The graduations in the auditorium were pathetic affairs. Diplomas were handed out as well as certificates for classes completed in cooking, painting, canning, and the like. Graduation was held on a holiday, with a program of music. The students came dressed in their best, their friends applauded heartily, and a synthetic "good time" was had by all. A new department, a sign of the automation era, was organized in Alderson shortly before I left. It was part of a national system, according to a Federal prison report for 1958, to keep a record of every federal prisoner—age, sex, race, citizenship, prison record, etc. The records went from all federal prisons to the National Training School for Boys, where tables and charts were prepared for official reports. A few inmates familiar with IBM operations were assigned to the code machines and trained others. It was quite amazing how much information these soulless machines leaked to prisoners. Secrecy is impossible in such a place.

While I was in Alderson prison I wrote several poems, if my amateurish efforts could be so dignified. It began in fun, to amuse my cottage mates. The first was called "Commissary Love." It was passed around quite generally, and the suggestion was made to submit it to the prison quarterly, *The Eagle*. To my surprise it was accepted and published in the Easter 1956 issue, signed Elizabeth F. But with the prudery of this hypocritical place, the title was changed to "Fickle Females," and the word love was changed to like, much to the amusement of all who had read it, including officers. Two others, "Sunset—A Mood in Cottage 26" and "Venus over Alderson," were also published in this issue. The one on the sunset was reprinted in the June 1956 issue of a religious paper distributed at the prison, called *The Happy Harvester*, published in Cleveland, Texas.

In the mid-Summer issue of the *Eagle*, July 1956, I had three items published, a poem called "Any Alderson Holiday," another called "House Hunting in Alderson" and an article on the Declaration of Independence, to which I appended the Four Freedoms of Franklin D. Roosevelt. How I came to write this was interesting. The officer in charge said, "Elizabeth, can you write a patriotic article for our 4th of July issue on the Declaration of Independence?" I replied I would try. I assembled my data from the *World Almanac* and several American histories. The undertaking pleased me, writing this behind prison bars. I was amazed that they accepted it. The prison magazine went to all other federal prisons and to the prison authorities in Washington. The article was signed Elizabeth F. But somehow Murray Kempton found out about it and wrote in his column in the *New York Post* of July 31, 1956, as follows:

"Miss Elizabeth Gurley Flynn, who was convicted under the Smith Act during the campaign year 1952, has been in a West Virginia Federal Prison for women. Last July 4th the prison authorities asked her to write a patriotic editorial. Neither she nor they seemed to think it odd for a July 4th

piece to come from a woman convicted of conspiracy to advocate the overthrow of the government of the United States;
she wrote it and they printed it. She is regarded by all parole
boards as unrepentant and therefore unfit for mercy; she is
only fit to tell federal prisoners why they should love America. I would like to say that Thomas Jefferson would have
been proud of this story; but I am more sure that he would
have wondered what she was doing in jail in the first place.
Jefferson, bless him, was better than most of us because he had
no need for the sense of irony."

My sister Kathie was disturbed lest her writing privileges
would be jeopardized by this disclosure. She called him up
and he reassured her. He said someone from Texas had called
it to his attention.

[11]

Back to Cottage 26

Easter Sunday was my first holiday in prison. It brought a
sudden change in our lives at Davis Hall No. 2. On Good Fri-
day we were notified to get ready to move on Saturday. That's
how things happened there. We had heard rumors of this for
some time. Cottage 26 had been painted and cleaned. Orientation had been moved to downstairs in Davis Hall. The
number of inmates was steadily increasing and the whole of
this building was now needed. Easter dinner was a surprise.
Only on holidays or when the Parole Board came did we
have such fare. I helped cut out, print, and color egg-shaped
menus which read as follows: "Baked ham with raisin sauce,
mashed potatoes, lettuce wedges with mayonnaise, buttered
asparagus, bread, ice cream, and coffee." For a special treat

women were allowed to smoke at the table. On Sunday I went to the auditorium to hear the fine singing of an interracial choir, interspersed with piano and organ solos.

Meantime, we had packed all our belongings and trekked back to the little cottage next door. I was assigned a small room, formerly used for lock-ins. It was on the dark side ground floor, with barred windows. At least it had a welcome private toilet and wash bowl. It was across the hall from rooms occupied by officers and three doors from the office, so I was still under maximum surveillance. The cottage was in a small hollow. My window looked out on a park with a rock garden, full of beautiful spring flowers in bloom. The room was too small to work in, so I took my sewing to the large room we had used in our orientation days. In warm weather I sewed on a small back porch, looking out on the river, the mountains, and the railroad. Later this was not allowed. Mercifully, the radio was then in the small living room, at the other end of the hall. Four of us on the ground floor were allowed to use showers in the basement. This was due to the fact that A, my Negro woman friend now next door to me, was not allowed to go upstairs, to avoid trouble with others. The officer was expected to keep an eye on her at all times. At first she was dissatisfied because her special girl friend was upstairs. But Miss Jones, then the assistant warden, talked to her. The only other inmate downstairs at the time was an elderly Irish-American woman, who was also kind to her. "Aren't you going to get along just fine here," Miss Jones said, "with only Elizabeth and K? It's just like a private suite." I had to smile. But she became quite satisfied and we settled down in our new quarters.

The Irish woman had been sent to us from orientation because she was too ill to go to a regular cottage. She felt deeply humiliated to be among "such people." She suffered to hear bad language. To her it was horrible that I was there too, and she could not understand how I could be friendly with the others. She had been involved in some financial troubles relative to her father's estate, by illegally possessing herself of the entire amount, secreting it from her mother and daughter, contending they were unfit to handle it. It was obvious she was not a thief, but a stubborn, self-willed woman, who had ruled her family with an iron hand. Advised by the priest, her parole officer, and lawyer, she finally agreed to make a proper restitution to her estranged family. After a court settlement she was paroled.

But her punishment took another unhappy form. One day, while she was awaiting her release, another inmate rushing down the stairs with her arms full of laundry, bumped into her causing her to slip and fall on the highly waxed floor. She fractured her shoulder blade, it would not heal, and she left with her arm in a sling, threatening to sue the Bureau of Prisons. My little blonde friend had caused the accident. She cried, helped the injured woman to the hospital, and felt very badly. But it became apparent from the questions she and others of us were asked, that an attempt was being made to charge that she had deliberately injured the other woman and thus save the institution from a possible suit for damages. We were all very indignant and K too insisted it was an accident.

Cottage 26 was physically better for us than Davis Hall. There was more space and light and a large backyard to play ball and hang clothes. But I saw few other prisoners except my cottage mates. The strain was very great at times. I realized that some of the women were dangerous mental cases who should have been in other institutions. Only if they became either continuously violent or depressed to the point that they knew no one, or did not know where they were or what they were doing, were they sent to St. Elizabeth's Hospital in Washington, D.C. One borderline case was an Indian woman, who had a violent temper and suffered delusions that she had had a baby there which had been taken away from her. She claimed that one of the guards came to her room at nights. This was the only cottage, the maximum security, where the night watchwoman officer was accompanied by a male guard, which caused her to make this charge. We all discussed with her which boy friend she should marry after her release, and it helped keep her calm.

One day I walked to commissary with her. She said she had cancer of the face (of which I could see no trace) because her husband had struck her there repeatedly. Shocked, I said: "How dreadful. You should have done something about it." She replied, "I did. I killed him!" The woman laughed and insisted it was true and that she had served a prison term for it.

As time passed the rules were gradually relaxed in my case. This was due not to any decisions by higher-ups but mainly to cottage officers, who could not understand the severity. One officer said: "You need exercise, Elizabeth. Sweep the porch and walk, in front of the cottage." I sat on a low stone wall to rest, chatting with passers-by. It was a joy to be out in the sunshine and to put my feet on the earth. It relieved the monotony of hours of sewing and the eye strain I was beginning to feel. If I saw a top officer coming I'd get very busy with my broom. I volunteered to polish the doorknobs and did an especially good job on the brass eagle knocker on the front door. The inmates swore they could hear the eagle scream in protest. I recalled the Gilbert and Sullivan operetta of a guy who "polished up the knocker on the big front door and now I am captain of the Queen's Navy." I aspired to no such reward.

I missed having a writing table in my cubbyhole of a room. There was no room for a bureau, only the small metal chests of orientation days. We were given long boxes on wheels, like a sailor's chest or a soldier's footlocker. They went under the bed and held all the extra belongings. An officer gave me a one-armed chair which I used for a desk. One day the Warden came through, inspecting. She demanded to know where I got the chair. I pretended I did not remember which officer gave it to me, much to the officer's relief. They all stood in awe of Miss Kinzella. She decreed it belonged in the school building and they would send for it. But they never came and I passed it on to someone else when I left that cottage.

We had hoped that medical motions pending in court on behalf of Claudia Jones and elderly Jacob Mindel would be decided favorably. But what one judge had called "the therapeutic value of prison routine" prevailed. In early April the motions were denied. I knew later one has to be at the point of death for such a release. Even then the wait may be too long. In Alderson I heard a woman called "a malingerer" who died a few weeks later in St. Elizabeth's Hospital. I have seen prisoners brought in on stretchers and in wheelchairs and others taken out in ambulances.

But the silver lining to my cloud was that Claudia Jones was now moved from a segregated cottage to 26. Judge Dimock had ordered that she must have a salt-free diet. At first they claimed it was impossible at Alderson. But when he threatened to release her, they found it could be done. Davis Hall kitchen, which provided all the hospital diets, also fed us. Claudia was sent a special tray for each meal. She was assigned a vacant room two doors from me, on the other side of A, my Negro woman friend, who welcomed her gladly. She remained there until she left in October 1955.

I can never forget my joy at seeing her in the doorway, with friends helping carry her things. It changed my life in prison for that period. She worked days in the craft shop weaving. She made over 30 beautiful colored tablecloths for the staff dining room. She became interested in all the crafts taught there—ceramics, pottery, metal jewelry, wood carving, and leather work. Miss Helen Smithson, in charge of the craft shop, refused to be classified as a custodial officer and was officially designated as an occupational therapist and teacher. She told me later that Claudia was the most talented pupil she ever had. It was remarkable, since Claudia had never done any of these things before.

Her absorption in the many projects helped pass the time

more quickly. Even when in the hospital, she did clay modelling. She set up a small loom in her room and wove a centerpiece and matching place mats of white and gold thread, which won a prize at the local county fair. Years ago, when Dr. Harris was the warden, the prison held its own fair. Now there were only numbers on the articles and nothing to show they were prison-made. Claudia taught several girls in our cottage to model in clay, and another to play the piano enough to encourage her to take lessons from the music teacher. In the evening we would discuss, read our letters to each other, exchange news of the day. We were sorry Betty was so far away down the hill, and knew she must be lonely. Dorothy Rose Blumberg had since gone home. Claudia's room was next to the office. Inmates came to us for help and advice more than to the officers. In fact, the latter often sent them to us, in many cases.

Sunday afternoon was called "the quiet hour." After lunch everyone was locked in to rest. Some went to church later. But one could stay locked in until the evening meal. Most came out as soon as possible because few women in prison are self-sufficient. They crave company, talk, the radio, cards, dancing, excitement. However, Claudia and I usually rested all afternoon.

One Sunday, just before July 4th, the key turned in my door. Miss Kinzella, her assistant, and a strange man stood there. He said: "Good afternoon. Weren't you expecting us?" I replied, "No, who are you, please?" He answered, "I am James Bennett, head of the Federal Bureau of Prisons." I did not want Miss Kinzella to introduce me, I knew she would simply say, "This is Elizabeth." So I replied quickly: "I'm glad to meet you, Mr. Bennett. I am Elizabeth Gurley Flynn, of the Communist Party." He looked slightly surprised, but said, "Oh, yes. We have had some correspondence, I believe."

We had a brief conversation about our trial, the present status of our appeal. There had just been the first dissenting opinion in a Smith Act case by Judge Hastie of Pennsylvania.

Mr. Bennett noticed my dead son's picture. "Do I know this gentleman?" he asked. I said that possibly he mistook him for Eugene Dennis. The resemblance was quite striking. He asked me how I spent my time, what I did, what I wrote, did I write poetry? This gave me the opportunity to present my one big problem, my need of paper for writing. He said I could write all I pleased, but I could not take any written material out unless it was checked by his office. However, he told Miss Kinzella to permit me to order 500 sheets of paper through commissary. I told him Claudia was two doors away and he visited her, inquiring about her health and diet. We felt that these unsolicited visits indicated an involuntary recognition of our true status as "politicals" and the inquiries of a large number of people as to how we were being treated.

Possibly, I should have registered a protest against being held in maximum security. I refrained because I did not want to be separated from Claudia. I ordered the paper and received it two months later, in September. I put a notice on the box in my bureau, "Allowed to me by Mr. Bennett. Do not touch," so that some officer would not confiscate it as contraband, in a "shake down." It lasted until I left and not a single sheet was stolen. Only a person who writes can appreciate what a joy it was to me, even if I could not take any writings out.

The Fourth of July was a festive occasion, possibly due to Mr. Bennett's presence. There was a chicken dinner and a bottle of Coca-Cola for each woman. I gave mine away in deference to our French comrades, who despise the stuff. In many European countries Coca-Cola is identified with the American take-over—the Marshall Plan and what followed. I was at a banquet in Paris in 1950, celebrating the 80th birthday of Marcel Cachin, Editor of the Communist Party daily paper, *l'Humanite*. The waiter, ready to pour champagne for me, said humorously: "Maybe the American comrade would prefer Coca-Cola?" I hastened to assure him I never drank it, which was true then and now. He had been a waiter in New York City at the Waldorf-Astoria Hotel.

On the July 4th holiday in Alderson there were foot races and a baseball game on the lower campus. Many of the younger girls were excellent players. A prize was given to the cottage with the most original costume. To the surprise of everyone, the stepchild of the prison, our much despised maximum security cottage, won the prize, thanks to Claudia Jones. She had gathered an enthusiastic group around her, which worked for days on the costumes fashioned to illustrate the popular song, Davy Crockett. She went through all the theatrical costumes in the school stores and selected Indian and scout attire, and put signs on others. All but a few scornful anti-social individuals in the cottage participated and enjoyed the fruits of victory, candy and cigarettes. The women carefully cleaned, mended, and pressed all the garments before returning them to the storehouse. Claudia had demonstrated what a little effort could do to create a healthy group pride and cooperation in what was considered the most backward cottage on the reservation.

August 7, 1955, was my 65th birthday. It was celebrated inside and remembered outside of Alderson. Kathie had sent out letters notifying a great many people, friends, acquaintances, and others who knew of me. Messages poured in to Alderson, but they were not given to me, although they made quite an impression.

Among those which Kathie received and which I treasured was this one: "Loving birthday greetings, dear Elizabeth Flynn. May the sense of serving mankind bring strength and peace into your brave heart. Affectionately Helen Keller."

Another was from Sean O'Casey: "Dear friend, Irish, and, at least, not ashamed of it. I understand you reached your 65th birthday on August 7th of this year. I am one who is on his way to his 76th birthday—am sending you a sincere greeting, wherever you may be—in jail or out of it. It is, in my opinion, nonsense to think of you as any but a brave and a noble woman, who, like most of the artists and poets and thinkers who give new resolution to life, stood by that principle that all men are born equal, and so should have equal opportunity to live a full life. It is not this man or that man who owns the world, but all men and all women who own the right to make the most of what the world can give them, that life however hard, may have a golden light around it. Even where you are at the moment, in whatever kind of what is called a cell, this light steals through and lingers around the heart of the brave and good woman—Elizabeth Gurley Flynn. My dear greetings to you, Irish one, and my love too. Yours very sincerely—Sean O'Casey."

Kathie wrote me that Dr. Clemens France had sent her a shawl from Galway, Ireland, which was a family heirloom. As our mother was born in Galway, this gift was deeply appreciated and Kathie kept it safely for me until I came home. She wrote me of innumerable other birthday greetings, all of which she saved along with articles in newspapers and magazines. The girls in the cottage gave me little gifts, a greeting signed by all of them, and they sang "Happy Birthday." So another milestone was passed, a birthday in prison.

[12]

I Go "Underground"

In a few months I had sewed, mended, and labelled everything available in the cottage. In addition to my assigned work I kept busy with volunteer work for inmates who could not sew or did not want to do so. I turned up hems of aprons and dresses, made dresses smaller, and according to style books turned loose fitting shirts into trim Eisenhower jackets for members of the paint crew, who were allowed to wear them for safety. All alterations and decorations had to be ripped out before the garments went back to the supply room. Embroidery had to be taken off, buttons sewed on, patches made, and I did this too for inmates getting ready to go out. I found a lot of waste material stored in the basement and made ruffled covers for the iron chests, to make them look like vanity tables. But try as I would, I could not keep myself busy. Then someone came up with a bright idea.

The woman who had done the hospital mending had gone home and things had piled up over there. I was assigned to do it. The head nurse came to tell me what they needed done and bundles of work were brought over. Nurses' aprons, doctors' white coats, operating gowns, sheets, pillowcases, were to be mended. They wanted belts made to feminize the government hospital bathrobes. She asked me to do a rush job by hand on babies' belly bands. I thought such things were long since discarded in modern hospitals, but "mine is not to reason why." I made them from a very soft material. One of the officers helped. When the girls saw her sewing them they teased her, "Why Mrs. B we didn't know you were expecting!"

Next it was decided to set up a private sewing room for me in the basement where the orientation examination room had been. There was a good linoleum floor, a wash bowl, a large closet for my materials, a long worktable and several comfortable chairs. In an adjoining room were two showers and a toilet. Two large windows, barred of course, looked out on the mountains, to the West. An electric sewing machine was brought over from the hospital, which I learned to use by attending the sewing class. It was a strange arrangement, but I liked it. I was completely alone, locked in, except for the lunch hour. Other inmates were not allowed down except by special permission. The reasons given were that no one else was permitted to use the machine and the hospital goods might be stolen. Also, articles to be returned to the clothing room were stored there. Undoubtedly, it was also to further isolate me from the other inmates. I joked about "going underground" and asked if I could move my bed and things and live down there. It would have been a nice little apartment.

One day, an assistant warden came to ask me if I could make pillows. She said a number of inmates, including some in the hospital, were allergic to feathers. There was a large supply of kapok in the storehouse, from the borders of tow targets and parachutes which were ripped up for nightgowns and underwear. They brought a supply to me, also a large bolt of ticking, and gave me the necessary measurements. The sewing teacher showed me how to adjust the machine for heavy material, and I was in the pillow business. I made at least 50 pillows before the kapok gave out and no more was forthcoming. They piled up on the table and I carried on a campaign, nagging at the officers to get them to the hospital. Two of us could have carried them over. But the cottage officers had no authority to order this. The hospital and the prison (under different government departments) carried on a running jurisdictional dispute. Under prison red tape the pillows had to go to the storehouse and be requested by the hospital. I do not know what kind of hassle went on between two government departments about my pillows. But when I left that cottage in December, months later, they were still there. One day I met the assistant warden who had given me the pillow task. Apparently, she had forgotten it. But I reminded her they were still in the basement of Cottage 26. She got busy and finally they were distributed to the suffering "allergics." Another example of frustrating prison red tape!

I rarely had an outside visitor in my "underground." But one day a shadow fell over my work and I looked up. Officers were always able to move silently. This time it was Miss Kinzella, a tall, straight-backed, grey-haired woman, prim and distant. The gulf between her and the inmates was unbridgeable. I was told she came to her present position from a secretarial post in Mr. Bennett's office and had no training for prison work. She impressed me as an inarticulate woman, very unsure of herself. I had caught a large black water bug and put it in a wash bowl of hot water. She asked me where I found it and if I had a piece of paper to wrap it in. I had a small brown paper bag and she went out, carrying it gingerly. Next day the sanitation squad came to fumigate. I had to abandon my work room temporarily. When I returned later I found a little field mouse there, so desperate for water he came right up to me in the shower. I poured water on the floor, which he drank feverishly and waited for more. Next day I found him dead, apparently a victim of the fumigation.

During most of the time I was in Alderson I went each week to the sewing class. It was a diversion, in a pleasant room attached to a big modern kitchen, where the cooking classes were held. Inmates sat around, chatting freely. The teacher was tolerant of the conversations and a relaxed atmosphere prevailed. The course required students to first make an apron and a nightgown, which went to the institution. Then we could make a dress to measurements and keep it for personal use by turning in one of our other dresses. I made myself a grey dress and later a green one. In the advance class I bought material and made three smocks for Kathie. Many inmates bought material and made their own going-out outfits, a subject of great interest in the sewing room.

One of the oddest requests I had was from an officer in Cottage 26 to make a pair of "falsies" for a sick inmate, who was painfully thin, flat as a pancake, and who brooded over her lack of shape. The officer brought me an old silk nightgown, which was strictly against the rules, and some stiffening. We contrived to build a special brassiere quite nicely. It helped the poor thing's morale considerably. Another girl asked me to reinforce her prison brassiere so she could pull it in and flatten her breasts. She desired to look as masculine as possible. I refused and warned her of the danger of cancer from breast injuries. She replied flippantly, "Well, they'll have to cut them off then!" I made it a rule not to alter slacks or shirts so as to masculinize them. Some wanted them narrowed to Mexican-like trousers, even with black stripes down the sides. The girls laughed at my scruples but did not insist.

Eventually, I again worked myself out of a job. I had very little sewing to do. I stretched it out as long as possible, so I could stay in my basement. I read and wrote letters there and kept up the pretense of sewing, if a strange officer appeared. I covered chairs, made curtains to brighten up the cottage. I repeatedly asked for more kapok, as I had plenty of ticking and could have made many more pillows. But none came. Eventually, the room was closed and I was upstairs again, given cottage assignments, as before. One reason was that a crew of men came to build a high fence around the backyard. No woman, young or old, was allowed within talking distance of a man, except the priest. It took them all Summer to build the metal fence. When it was completed a girl climbed up quite easily and ran away from Cottage 26. Such episodes created great hilarity throughout the prison population.

While the men who were prisoners from a nearby institution, worked there, the officers had their hands full. Some girls dropped notes from the windows. When caught they were sent to seclusion. The foreman guard would pick up the notes and turn them over to our officers. One girl had to be moved to the other side of the house. She would talk to the men, "propositioning" in awful language which embarrassed all around.

[13]
The Difference

One of my correspondents asked me: "What do you think are the main differences between a women's prison and a men's prison?" I replied: "You would never see diapers hung on a line at a men's prison or hear babies crying in the hospital on a quiet Sunday afternoon." The physiological differences—menstruation, menopause, and pregnancy—create intense emotional problems among many women in prison. They certainly are far less restrained than men who are curbed by standards of manliness and do not want to be considered cry-babies or sissies by their fellow prisoners. Women just don't give a darn. To weep, have hysterics, shriek, scream, have "spells," are expected behavior patterns among women in prison. To be self-controlled, keep your chin up, be a good sport, be able to take it—is expected of men, in daily life, in the army, and in prison. But women are deaf to such appeals. They don't care if they are undisciplined, childish, unreasonable. In fact, one officer told me, "If we can keep them quiet, it's about all we are able to do." There is the story of a girl who ran complaining to an officer, "Mary told me to drop dead." The weary officer replied: "Alright, only do it quietly."

This generalization is not to say that there are not some adult and mature women in prison, who exercise self-control and quietly make the best of their trying ordeal. But there was constant tension among six hundred strange women, thrown together in the closest proximity, torn from husbands, children, homes, work, and mode of life, whatever it had been. They were frustrated and unhappy, resented everything there and expressed their rebellion in every possible way, including noise. I did not blame them, though I suffered from the noise. I'd hate to see them cowed and submissive, but I did often wish their emotions could be channelized in some quieter ways. I understood how they hated the place and literally beat their heads, "bloody but unbowed," against all restrictions. They even hated the scenery. "Damned country," they would complain.

The women in prison were certainly much more concerned about their appearance than men would be. They were fearful of aging too fast, particularly those with long sentences. This was the major topic of absorbing interest to a large number; they kept busy with hairdo's, manicuring, cold creaming faces and arms, getting suntans in Summer, reducing or putting on weight. Many came in with short hair but there was no provision for keeping it short and neat. Men had barber shops in prison; the women should have had a beauty parlor. It would have been a real morale builder. There was talk of installing one, but when I left it had not materialized. Inmates were allowed to cut each other's hair, but if it came out too short, like a man's, it was a disciplinary. There were plenty of shorn heads just the same, and even some sidelocks, to look like Elvis Presley. Many women came in with dyed hair. I recall one who was a platinum blonde, a disguise which helped her elude arrest for quite a while. These women were a messy sight until the hair grew out to its natural color, which all too often was grey or white. It took months to get rid of the patches of dyed hair, which was very embarrassing. They would say to visitors, especially husbands, "Look how I'm turning grey in here!"

The women usually tried to dress up for special occasions, church, visitors, graduations. They bought plain handkerchiefs at commissary and embroidered them or crocheted deep lace borders and butterflies on one corner. They knitted or crocheted attractive little caps, to wear to Catholic services. They ironed pleats into the plainest dresses and even made tatting to sew around collars and cuffs. With pretty-colored sweaters and earrings and pins, all made there, it was amazing how well-dressed they could look. The bad feature, which caused angry grief, were the socks, and the ugly prison-made shoes. If each woman could have had just one nice pair of shoes for dress-up wear, it would have given them all a tremendous lift.

A ridiculous struggle went on to force the women to wear slips. They were sent back to their cottages from all places, to put them on, and it was made a disciplinary. If they had been allowed to wear half-slips they probably would not have objected so much. But the shoulder straps of bras and slips were cumbersome at work. Most of them did not wear slips outside. They considered them old-fashioned and complained that there was no reason for them in a place habitated only by women. "Fussy old maids," they called the officers who demanded slips.

Pregnant women were given special diets, light work, and their health was checked regularly. One Negro woman from the South, who had eight children, told me that this was the first time she had had a doctor's care. Classes for prospective mothers were held in the craft shop, where they made baby shoes and bibs of soft white leather. Sometimes there would be seven or eight women, Negro and white, big with child, sitting around the table. As the time of birth approached the expectant mothers with their night clothes in a little bundle, would go to the hospital to sleep, returning in the early morning to their cottages. This was to avoid an emergency during the night, when all were locked in. I wrote a poem about pregnant women in the shop and another about two who passed daily by my window in the dusk of evening and in the morning. "To The Prison Madonnas" was published in the *Eagle*.

The mothers were allowed to take their new babies back to the cottage for a few months. Husbands or families could take the baby home, or, if they were unable to come, an officer was sent with the baby. In former years the children stayed for two or three years. But officers claimed the young children "jiggered" for inmates, as standing watch is called in prison. Now that was over. In a few instances a mother rejected the baby, refusing to see it. Some were very young, unmarried, or the victims of rape. These children were placed for adoption. The presence of a baby in a cottage was a pleasant humanizing influence. The women fed it, watched over it, knitted caps, sweaters, booties. They criticized a mother who failed to take proper care of her baby.

Mothers and babies were kept in the "food cottages," in which there were kitchens and dining rooms serving three cottages. The mother was assigned to prepare food so she could be there at all times. Occasionally, a cottage officer would bring the baby to the dining room, to show the women of other cottages. The "ohs and ahs" expressed their admiration. The parting of mother and child, especially if she faced a long sentence, was heartrending. The grief and worry of these poor women affected their health and spirits, sometimes to the point of collapse. Certainly, in these cases, there should be some special parole provisions, especially for first offenders, to keep the mother and baby together.

Another manifestation of femininity were the attempts to decorate the rooms with pictures, plants, a few books, even if they never read them. Large empty wax cans masqueraded as stools or smoking tables, attempts at altars were made by the more devout, old papers and magazines accumulated, until the rooms became so cluttered a general cleanup was ordered. All extraneous things were removed. The library sent out a call for books long overdue. Dozens were gathered up. Neglected plants, needing water and sun, were confiscated. Towels held out to make table covers, extra pillows covered as sofa pillows, extra rugs beyond the two allowed, all had to be turned in on pain of a disciplinary, amidst loud lamentations.

It was amazing what odd things turned up in these "shakedowns." Little round boxes, used originally for typewriter ribbons were used as ashtrays; empty flower pots, cold cream jars, spoons and knives from the kitchen, extra glasses, large jars for water, vases. Extra clothes were always described as "loaned by a friend." A girl who worked in the clothing room was found to have 15 dresses. She was sent to seclusion. Everything that could not be accounted for as legitimate, which meant issued by the institution or purchased in commissary, was confiscated. All heavy articles, which could be used as weapons, were declared contraband. After a siege of drinking glasses being smashed wholesale in Cottage 26, we were given plastic cups and all glasses were removed.

Borrowing was one of the most troublesome habits. It was almost impossible to get back what you loaned. You treasured your few irreplaceable possessions, lent them with caution and insisted on their return. On departure inmates gave them away, sometimes to friends, occasionally to the needy. There was a waiting line for everything. Requests were made months in advance. It was pathetic to see what an old sweater, mittens, a scarf, a few handkerchiefs, meant to women who had nothing except prison issue.

To get the operational work done at Alderson and save the expense of civilian labor, the prison authorities disregarded physiological differences and had many women prisoners doing what is ordinarily called "men's work" outside. An example was the assignment of inmates on the coldest days to clean the long flight of steps, "the 64's." Ice accumulated, and a crew was sent out to chip and clear it off. One girl from Florida who had no rubbers, mittens, or scarf came into the craft shop to warm up. She was blue with the cold. Girls loaned her the articles she needed to face the icy wind.

However, no special compensation or consideration, such as extra rest periods, was forthcoming. This was notably true of the paint crew, who worked all the year around. In the Winter they painted the insides of the cottages, the school, administration building, barns at the dairy, the warden's house, officers quarters, even outside the reservation. They even painted the large and high ceilinged auditorium. In Summer they painted the outsides of all the buildings, climbed forty-foot ladders to reach the upper garret windows. They had no vacations, in fact, no inmate, not even lifers, had vacations. Two days a month was allowed off, presumably for menstrual periods. Thousands of dollars in painters' wages were saved by the labor of these hard-working women, who had a civilian boss, a man who directed them. Ostensibly all prison work was supposed to train women for outside work. But it was not so in this instance. Women are not employed as painters, they are not eligible to the unions, and few would want to do such work.

Women ran the dairy, the piggery, the farm, the garment shop, the laundry, maintenance work in the cottages, taking care of the lawns, etc. Other jobs that were particularly heavy were in the storehouse and on the trucks, which carried supplies all over the place. They entailed lifting, loading, and delivering heavy articles—food stuffs for the kitchens, paints and other fluids to the paint crew, boxes of thread, leather hides and metal to the craft shop; bolts of goods to the garment shop; medical supplies to the hospital; office supplies to clerical forces; wax, cleaning fluids, soap, toilet paper and Kotex to the cottages. Everything for the work of the entire institution passed through the storehouse. All the handling was done by women. This would certainly be considered men's work outside.

Betty Gannett worked in the storehouse during her entire stay from January 1955 to September 1956. Her aptitude tests demonstrated that she was a skilled typist, teacher, writer. Yet all that could be found for her at Alderson was hard manual labor. She was neither young nor strong, though with an unconquerable spirit. She demanded and secured the change in the storehouse that two women, not one, should carry the 100-pound sacks. This task was injurious to women and could interfere with child-bearing later. She suffered a deep ugly cut on her leg when a large can of peanut butter fell on it. By November 1955 her weight had diminished from 127 pounds to 111 and she was suffering from severe arthritis. She had requested a change in work assignment and was finally, after a long struggle, transferred to clerical work at a desk in the storehouse of such a minor character that she was practically idle.

This was irksome and embarrassing to Betty, since everyone around her was working at top speed. The head dietician asked for Betty's transfer to her department but it was refused. Betty then requested to be returned to her former work, which was promptly granted. This failure to assign her to suitable work, forcing her to toil beyond her strength, was obviously discrimination against a political prisoner.

That this charge is not exaggerated is evident from the treatment she was accorded from the beginning. The initial medical examination was so cursory that the doctors failed to find anything wrong, although she suffered from angina. For months they failed to check on heart pains and an arthritic condition. Only after a new young doctor came to Alderson was she finally given a Masters' Test which verified damage to the heart and a condition of angina pectoris. After eleven months of neglect by previous doctors, he recommended a change of work. The desk job was the result.

When Betty's family came to see her, a rule that conversations must be carried on in the English language was enforced. Her oldest brother could not speak English without a considerable use of Jewish words. So the poor old man was not allowed to talk to her at all. The excuse was they had to check on "conspiracy" under the Smith Act. On meritorious good time for constructive work done in a prison, Betty had a good conduct rating, had established seniority in the warehouse, and was proficient. Others with less seniority, received good time. But she, like other politicals, was denied it.

When she was returned to the hard manual labor job the second time, both her attorney, Mrs. Kaufman, and her husband, James Tormey, began insistent pressures in Washington with the Bureau of Prisons and she was finally returned to the desk job, but this time with some appropriate work to do. She remained there till she came out, nine months later, with her health badly impaired. On the matter of visits, in March 1956, James Tormey objected to the Warden and to Mr. Bennett against the extremely insulting supervision given to his visits to his wife and against the prohibition of her brother's conversation. In reply to a letter from Mrs. Kaufman, Mr. Bennett's reply was as follows:

DEAR MRS. KAUFMAN:

I have your letter of March 8, 1956, concerning the supervision of visits between Miss Betty Gannett and her husband, Mr. James Tormey.

I should like to say at the outset that we consider visits to inmates a privilege. We have always reserved the right to approve visitors and to determine the conditions and degree of supervision under which visits may be held. With respect to Miss Gannett, the visits are more closely supervised than are those of many other inmates. On the other hand, there are and have been many inmates whose visits have been just as closely supervised and these persons have been convicted of a variety of offenses. I therefore cannot concede that she is being discriminated against. By the nature of the offense for which she was convicted, conspiracy to teach and advocate the overthrow of the United States Government by force and violence, it is incumbent upon us to see that she does not engage in any way in the continuance of this offense while she is serving her sentence.

Under the circumstances I find no reason to change the visiting practices in effect.

Very truly yours,
(*signed*) JAMES V. BENNETT
Director.

[14]

Women Prison Officers

Undoubtedly, there were differences between women officers in Alderson and men guards in other prisons. The majority of the cottage officers were local women, with families in the nearby communities. They were extremely dependent on their jobs since there are no industries employing women in this remote mountain area. Some had children in school, teenagers preparing for college, invalid husbands, or aged parents. One officer was mistaken for an inmate by a new prisoner. She asked, "What are you here for?" The officer replied, "Checks." The girl asked, "How long?" and she replied, "As long as they last." All were anxiously waiting for pensions. They are not too well paid. Correctional officers are listed in the Federal Prison report of 1958 as drawing $4,490 a year as starting salary, or $86 a week. This is for men; the women probably get less.

The officers were not trained penal workers, though some were trained nurses. They dreaded the annual examinations, and checked with us if they had answered correctly. Some of the most sensible and humane officers would fail. It was difficult to induce young single women to stay there very long. They felt they too were in prison. There were few places off the reservation to live comfortably, no places to go, not much social life, no chance to meet eligible men. One Midwesterner said to me, "Think I want to marry and support one of those hillbillies, like these fool women do here." Some younger women came for short periods, for institutional training, some to earn money for college. Some older ones who have been there ever since the prison opened, were obviously affected by the restricted life. They were ill at ease in the outside world on vacations, and hurried back to their cloistered life. They dressed in dowdy old-fashioned styles and were rated as eccentric or "a little off their rocker," by the inmates. If they were kind, the inmates were tolerant but if they were mean the women said, "They envy us because we've lived, and that's more than they have!" Some officers were quite ignorant of worldly ways, good or bad.

Although officers were not allowed to be abusive or use bad language and were not allowed to use force except in "self-defense," they could be very nasty; sarcastic, unfriendly, cold, austere, unreasonable, and demanding. There were many whom we all hated and despised as natural-born cops. They snooped and spied all the time, checked on every little infraction, were "pencil happy" or ready to write a disciplinary at a moment's notice. One who came to our cottage as a relief officer was so vicious that practically all the women locked in at seven o'clock to keep out of her way. These cop-officers would go into the inmates' rooms while they were at work, look over everything they possessed, read their letters, go over their personal papers, etc. They looked at us with distaste, spoke to us only when it was absolutely necessary, and treated us as if we were morons or children, never as equals.

Yet these exceptionally mean officers, who numbered about a fourth of those working on the reservation, also showed fear of us. I recall once going to the basement with one such who insisted I walk ahead of her down the stairs. "Expected you to konk her," the girls said. They were extremely unpopular with the prison population, who rated all officers and passed the word from cottage to cottage. Some who rated high were called dolls, dears, angels. Others were cops, rats, snitchers, bitches, if not worse. The inmates never came to the aid of cops, while they helped and covered up for the mistakes and shortcomings of a good officer. From the point of view of helping to rehabilitate, the cop-officers were complete failures. They created an atmosphere of tension, resistance, and hatred.

Four officers, at least, I recall were eccentric, one bordering on insanity. She would forget to lock doors and put out lights. Others were strict but decent and were rated as not too bad by the inmates. These numbered possibly half of the officers. A few, less than a dozen, were rated as tops—very good, and one or two were really loved by the inmates. My private rating of those who were intelligent or well-informed would be a scant handful at most. The one man, the priest, who was then on the staff, was helpful to all, regardless of religion. Seven were Negro officers, out of possibly 50 I can recall. They were efficient and intelligent, but forced to be disciplinarians because of prejudice against them. Only in Cottage 26 were the same officers allowed to remain indefinitely. Others were transferred around every few months, to avoid friendships between officers and inmates and the development of too great sympathy for the problems of prisoners.

The few who were "tops" were more like housemothers in a girls' school. They created a relaxed friendly atmosphere and cooperative relations. They would struggle with the administration to secure things which were needed in the cottage, better furniture, medical care for the sick, seasonable clothes, etc. They were rewarded for their efforts by appreciation and cooperation. The cottage officers on the lowest rungs of authority were in the most strategic position of daily contact with the prisoners. The work of rehabilitation should start with them. But they were barred by rules, were not allowed to take any initiative, and were supervised almost as much as the inmates. They were checked on continuously. If they went to the toilet and the telephone rang an imperious voice asked, if one of us answered the phone, "Where is your officer?" Only rarely would a message be left with an inmate. I always gave my name but usually the inmate answering said. "One of the girls." It sounded "like a whorehouse," one girl said.

Between the cottage officers and the Warden were a number of intermediaries; "straw bosses," working women called them. The cottage officers worked in two shifts. One came at six AM and left at two. The second came from two to ten PM. They did considerable work—checked the laundry out and in; doled out the mail and medicine; read the letters written in the cottage; distributed stationery, cleaning fluids, and all cottage supplies; checked inmates out and in. If all cottage inmates worked outside, the officer was assigned to help out at the hospital, craft shop, orientation, or elsewhere. They seldom had an idle moment. If they were good natured, they were drafted by the inmates to play cards.

Shortly after the regular officer left the cottage at night, another officer came to check on how she had left the cottage; living room, the showers, the storeroom, the medicine chest, office desks, electric lights. All our doors were tried to be sure the cottage officer had locked them. If the officer was good, the inmates made a check before she left and would call to her if she forgot a lock or a light. But they let a "cop" shift for herself. One officer told me she felt so humiliated it was all she could do to return each morning. Another officer who lived on the reservation, left in the middle of the night. One had resigned just before we came and went back to a police job in Florida. She said she was sick of the petty rules at Alderson. They had to pay for their meals, a nominal amount, but had to buy meal tickets in advance, for cash, after an officer's check bounced.

When we came to Alderson Negro officers were assigned almost entirely to the segregated cottages. In the Summer of 1955 a number were sent to Terminal Island, near Los Angeles, California, where a former immigration center was converted into a federal prison for both men and women. Quite a few women prisoners from Pacific and Western states and from Alaska, were also transferred there. After that no more prisoners came to Alderson from those areas. The Negro officers were not local women, their educational qualifications were superior to the whites, some had been in the armed services during the war. They told us of the hard time they had on their arrival in Alderson. Some white officers from the South quit rather than work with them. They were not permitted to eat in public restaurants in the town, even with white officers, and were handed their food in a bag to take out. One had been assigned to take charge of the piggery. She was a minister's daughter, a college graduate, and knew nothing of raising pigs. Practically all the women prisoners assigned to the piggery were Negroes. Before I left, the piggery was abolished.

After desegregation began in Alderson in 1955, following the Supreme Court decision, Negro officers were assigned in turn to all cottages. One came to Cottage 26. She was a widow with a small child. Her husband had been killed in the war. Some of the white inmates, led by the "Bandit Queen," threatened not to eat with her and not to obey her orders. Unfortunately, the white officer on the other shift encouraged them by her provocative conduct. When the Negro officer moved the garden tools out of the medicine chest and locked them in the storeroom, as dangerous, the white one ostentatiously moved them back again. Or when the Negro officer moved the office furniture on her shift, the white one moved it back. Such conduct between officers was unheard of. They usually hid their differences and worked together as a united front. Inmates began to take sides, and an ugly situation was brewing.

Claudia and I decided to take a hand in the situation. We talked to the Negro women inmates and the more reasonable among the whites, pointing out that she was entitled to the same respect as any other officer, and that she was being annoyed and harassed because of her color. They agreed to give her a courteous reception and told the others to lay off. She was very appreciative and unbent from her usual austere attitude to be cooperative and friendly. She was an accomplished musician, especially on the organ. Yet she was never asked to play for the institution. She played the piano in the cottage for us. She was very bitter, and we understood why. Claudia had many interesting conversations with her, especially if she was too severe with the women, pointing out that she should not take out her bitterness on helpless women, who were also victims of injustice in other ways. She kissed Claudia and shook hands with me when she left, an unusual courtesy from an officer to an inmate.

Claudia and I felt that having Negro officers was a half-hearted token business there at best. Desegregation was accompanied by a reduction in the number of Negro women officers. Those who were sent to Terminal Island were not replaced. One very fine Negro officer was suddenly dismissed. She was charged with allowing an inmate to use her key. But I heard it discussed in the craft shop by women from her cottage, who said it was not true, that trouble makers had accused her falsely to get rid of her. It could happen in Alderson. By the time I left I doubt if there were more than four Negro officers left. Only one was promoted to a higher grade and is now a parole officer, I understand.

[15]

Parole Bait

At the end of a third of one's sentence, application could be made for parole. Even during orientation, women began to plan how to proceed. It was a glimmer of hope, a will-o'-the-wisp, a snare and delusion, one of the refined cruelties connected with prison life. We helped a great many hopeful women prepare their applications and coached them in what to say to the Parole Board. Occasionally, to our surprise, our "client" made it. We learned a great deal about our fellow prisoners in the process. The majority were poor people, having little or no experience with legal procedure. Over half were either Puerto Ricans, not long from their native land and speaking little English, or Negroes, many from the deep South where they had no rights. I never met a Southern Negro woman who had voted. Few knew that they were supposed to be able to vote. The very thought of it seemed to frighten them.

Many prisoners, from all parts of the country, had been defended in an inadequate or shabby manner, by a court appointed or sometimes by a Legal Aid Society lawyer. I saw instances of this at Foley Square. Usually, the prisoners were advised to plead guilty and throw themselves on the mercy of the court. The judge asked a routine question, "Do you know what you are doing?" and inquired if any promises had been made to the prisoner, who always denied it emphatically. But what went on behind the scenes, between the client and an indifferent and disinterested lawyer, was another matter. The prisoner was led to believe that her lawyer had an understanding with the judge and prosecutor, that if the government was saved the expense of a trial her sentence would be light. I have seen women brought into the House of Detention and Alderson so stunned by ferocious sentences that they were in a state of shock, bordering on collapse.

I am not a lawyer, but I am certain there are many cases of double jeopardy where state and federal laws duplicate charges and sentences for the same offense, on the same show ᶜ evidence. I saw such a case where a woman had served ten rs in a Florida prison and then had to do time at Alderson. was completely penniless and was befriended only by a in the Florida prison hospital. I do not pretend to pass nt on the merits of each case, but some board of re- uld do so. The Parole Board does not. Some are undoubtedly guilty; a few frankly admit it. But I am convinced that a large number never had their day in court, were not presumed to be innocent until they were proven guilty, never had the benefit of a reasonable doubt, and were often the victims of callous neglect, plus popular and judicial prejudices.

I wish federal judges could hear how they were rated by inmates. If they could spend a short time incognito in a prison, it might make every judge, prosecutor, and parole officer a better administrator of justice. There was much resentment that sentences vary greatly for the same offense. There seemed no rule or reason. A judge might be dyspeptic or sadistic and there was no protection against his cruelty. There were justifiable grievances. One woman had a ten-year sentence and was released when two-thirds of her time expired. Another woman, on exactly the same charge, had a thirty-year sentence and could not apply for parole until she had served ten years. The state of public opinion can affect the length of sentences, as probably happened in these cases. Women who were serving time for forgery, theft, violation of drug or liquor laws, compared sentences and discovered extreme disparity. There is no prescribed uniformity of sentence, which causes anger and indignation on the part of those who have suffered a judge's wrathful severity, and from which there is no appeal if they pleaded guilty.

The Parole Board was supposed to be an instrument for relief but it did not work that way. They did not investigate the pre-sentence conditions, nor the justice of the sentence. They started with the assumption that the prisoner was guilty and must reform or rehabilitate, before parole can be granted. Parole is not a cancellation of sentence. It is not freedom. It is actually serving part of the sentence outside the prison, but under strict rules and supervision; and violations can cause return to prison on order of the parole officer, from which there is no appeal. It is a cat-and-mouse business, very nerve-racking and difficult to live by. The Board hearings were a source of anxiety, high hopes, and bitter disappointment. One or more Board members came regularly. After long service in such a capacity it was probably hard for them to listen with an open mind and without cynicism. They became case-hardened. The personnel should be changed often, to offset this. More women should be on the Parole Board. When we were first there the Board's arrival was signalized by the flag flying on every cottage. Later this was abandoned, maybe because it caused too much excitement on the reservation.

Applications had to be made several months in advance. They indicated that the prisoner has an outside parole adviser, possibly a minister, a former employer, or a local politician, but not a lawyer. A job had to be available for the applicant. Conditions of parole were strict. They limited travel, hours, residence, places frequented, and companions. Association with ex-convicts was strictly forbidden, except in cases of husbands and wives. Sometimes the violations seemed trivial or farfetched. One girl was returned to Alderson because she married without consent of her parole officer.

Days were spent figuring out what to say on the application and at the hearing. Hours were spent by applicants preparing for their appearance before the Board. Friends did their hair, lent them a sweater, a scarf, a fancy handkerchief. They wore their best dress. They practiced every word they planned to say. Everyone advised them and they would return to report in a most hopeful spirit. Claudia, Betty, and I were kept busy before the Parole Board came. Officers would say: "Go to Claudia and Elizabeth. They know all about those things!" I handled so much legal business—letters to lawyers, judges, and boards—I thought I'd be charged with practicing law without a license. In one case I drafted a touching letter for a girl to her pastor and to her judge, stressing her youth, her desire to reform, and pledged it would never happen again. To my surprise they both wrote to the Parole Board and she "made it." But to my chagrin, she sneaked over a state line to a tavern and was back again, in no time. However, George J. Reed, chairman of the U.S. Board of Parole, reported in December 1957 that 85 per cent of women parolees are good risks, a higher percentage than for men.

There were many obstacles to securing parole. Those who had pleaded guilty had one strike against them. Conduct in prison and work reports were checked, and officials consulted. Then there was a long wait until the Parole Board members returned to Washington and presumably made collective decisions. If it was a refusal a prison form came which merely said "Denied." No reasons were given, which was maddening. A period of despair, hysteria, anger and resentment followed. Any rehabilitation already under way was destroyed. Women stopped going to church saying, "What's the use?" and entered into a period of sullen brooding.

We could see no pattern in the denial in some cases and granting in others. There may be a yardstick, but from where we sat, it seemed arbitrary and haphazard. It looked as if more were released when the place became too crowded. There was no useful purpose in keeping the very young or mothers of families in prison, especially first offenders. First offenders on lesser charges were usually so chastened and frightened even in jail and certainly in prison, they were not likely ever to repeat the offense and could serve the balance of the term on parole, especially if they were not contaminated by prison ways. In a long period they were inevitably corrupted.

Much discussion ensued as to why some "made it." A cynical feeling prevailed that political influence came into play. The Board was certainly affected by routinism and callousness or timidity where a notorious case may have been involved. In 1958, approximately 68 per cent were denied parole in all federal prisons; 17 per cent of those sent back by parole officers were guilty of technical violations, 25 per cent were arrested in new infractions. Probably those denied were actually better risks than this 25 per cent whose alleged misdeeds were used to discredit the parole system, in sensational publicity.

The problem of recidivism or habitual criminality is bigger than the parole issue. What a challenge to the whole American penal system, with its claims of corrections, refor--mations, rehabilitations, that over 66 per cent of the men and women in prison are repeaters! It began at the prison gate when the stigma of ex-convict might as well have been stamped on the forehead. Readjustment to the outside world was difficult, at best, especially for those who have served long sentences. I have seen women afraid to ask for parole and frightened to face the day of release. Husbands have divorced them, families have disowned them, children have been taken away from them and grown up; they are as if resurrected from the dead, as unknown and unwanted as Enoch Arden.

The released prisoner needed help, especially financial, to tide her over the worst period. Instead she was given fare back to where she came from and a few dollars extra for food and lodging for a short period. In case one had funds, as we did, Uncle Sam gave nothing on departure. Is it strange then that the average ex-prisoner returned to old haunts and associates? There was no choice. If they were allowed to go to a strange city, change their names, helped to find a job and a decent place to stay, allowed to make new friends, rehabilitation would not be an empty phrase. Instead, ex-convicts are hounded by the police and FBI, rounded up every time a crime is committed in their vicinity, fired from jobs when employers are informed of their prison records. A parole officer may help a man or woman to secure a job and the FBI then comes around and gets them fired. Friendly aid to ex-convicts from police and detectives exists only in the fertile imagination of TV and radio script writers, who know little about it. It is extremely difficult, practically impossible, for ex-convicts to turn over a new leaf and go straight. This may explain the high degree of recidivism. I heard one young woman asked by an officer, "Would you commit the crime again?" She replied, "Yes, if my children were hungry again!"

No Smith Act prisoner was granted parole, though some applied. Betty and I had insisted Claudia should, on account of her health. But it was useless. As a political prisoner she asserted her innocence, her right to exercise her constitutional rights, and to be free and vindicated. She made none of the usual protestations of reformation. As we expected, she was denied.

There was, of course, a hard core of our prison population who were of the underworld. To them parole was a tactic, a stepping stone back to its ranks. They had no intention of changing their ways. Anyone outside their tight little circle was "a square," not to be trusted. They despised work and had contempt for workers. Unions were only to be exploited; crime was their occupation. They schemed and planned while there; how to get rich quick, have an easy and exciting life, cars, furs, jewels, live in good hotels, go South for the Winter, etc. Some few were clever high-class confidence women. Their aspirations sounded like those of many respectable ladies outside, wives of bankers, business men, and the like. Their tastes were similar.

A few in Alderson were reputed to be high up in the gang world. They had good lawyers, political connections; they were met at the gate by husbands or pals with big fancy cars, who scorned the cheap Alderson hotels. Some put up in the Green Briar Hotel at White Sulphur Springs nearby, to await their woman's coming out. One claimed proudly to be a niece of Al Capone, another boasted that she was a girlhood sweetheart of Lucky Luciano. Many were obviously small fry who often take "the rap" for the higher-ups without squealing, expecting their reward later. It would be a waste of time, I discovered, to discuss with them that their way of life is wrong and does not pay. They reflected the system that bred them and were convinced that "to get away with it" was the rule of life. For all their boastings of "big deals," some were the meanest chiselers in the prison. Others were generous to a fault, sharing everything. I met one such, a madam with a string of houses in a Southern city, which masqueraded as cocktail bars. While she helped the poor in Alderson she also did a little propaganda for her business, like, "See me outside, girls. I'll fix you up with a rich man!"

[16]

Alderson Under Dr. Harris

One day, browsing through the library, I found a book entitled, *I Knew Them in Prison*. Published in 1936, it was by Dr. Mary B. Harris, who had been the first Superintendent of Alderson, when it was called the Federal Industrial Institute for Women. It was amazing reading to an inmate of 1955. She described the building and early years of the institution. It was formally opened in 1928, as the first federal prison for women in the United States. Previously, the federal government had boarded out its women prisoners to state prisons, workhouses, and reformatories. As a prison without walls and generally without bars, it was considered a long step forward in penal reform. In the beginning years only first termers were admitted and recidivists and parole violators were sent elsewhere. This was considered an advantage for reform and rehabilitation of the accepted inmates.

The town of Alderson, which goes back to pre-revolutionary days, donated 200 acres and the government bought 300 more. They are at an altitude of 1600 feet. The climate is moderate, except for a short period in Winter. Water from the river is purified and filtered for use at the prison. The buildings are Georgian colonial style, built around two quadrangles called "the campuses." There is a sewage disposal plant, a central heating plant, electricity, good roads and side walks. It was planned as a small community within itself, with its own farm, dairy, greenhouse, school, chapel, library, auditorium, garment shop, laundry, bakery, and kitchens. Care was taken in building it, thanks to Dr. Harris, to preserve the beautiful trees—walnut, birch, oak, chestnut, maple, poplar, and evergreens. The cost of the building and equipment was two and one half million dollars.

It was originally planned to accommodate 500 inmates. When we were there the population was over 600. Cottages 26 and 27 were planned for quarantine and mental cases, therefore had barred windows. No other cottages had bars. They were named for women pioneers in prison reform. At first each cottage had its own kitchen and dining room. Then there were no dormitories. Each woman had her own room and an officer remained in the cottage at night. Apparently, a more domestic, less formal atmosphere prevailed.

Dr. Harris lists in her book the 21 organizations which attended a conference in Washington, D.C., in 1923, to promote the building of this institution. Practically every national woman's organization of that day was represented. (See Appendix 3 for the list.) It was held three years after women had won the right to vote, and their views had to be reckoned with. When the institution was formally opened many of these organizations sent representatives to participate. It would be well if these same organizations would check on the discrepancies between the original plans and the fine work of Dr. Harris as compared to the conditions at present. Practically all of her methods and ideas have been discarded. Her treatment of inmates as adult human beings has been abandoned. In her day, committees of women were set up in each cottage with a council of representatives who met regularly with Dr. Harris. New rules were discussed with them to secure their cooperation. Minor infractions were handled in the cottage by the groups, and were not subject to seclusion.

There was far less punishment than there is today and discipline was purposely inobtrusive. Some judges outside criticized Alderson because of this and claimed there was not enough correction. But Dr. Harris said in her book that attempts to escape were reduced, prisoners felt better understood, and seclusion was resorted to only when all else failed. Fighting and refusing to work were the main causes for seclusion then.

In sharp contrast to the dull routine of 1955, Dr. Harris was a great believer in activities. They had horses, cows, chickens, pigs, cats, and dogs on the reservation. There were Bird and Tree Clubs, Sunrise Bird Walks, an annual fair at the prison, a Christmas Bazaar, dances, plays, community singing, music teaching, child care training classes, all calculated to keep women busy and happy and to stimulate healthy discussions. She called all this "a safety valve." One inmate referred to it as "the goingest place I ever saw."

Dr. Harris was also a believer in preventing crises, by knowing each inmate personally, trying to meet them half way in their problems, thus reducing tension. Lifers who remember her swear by her, older officers wistfully pine for the good old days under her. As a result of her methods an inmate was rarely transferred from Alderson except as a mental case, as many so-called "incorrigibles" were when we were there. Nor was any woman placed in permanent isolation in her day, as we saw done. Under Dr. Harris a Personality Clinic was conducted by the record clerk, Miss Hironimus, a graduate lawyer, who succeeded Dr. Harris as Warden later. This was defined as a rational attempt at rehabilitation and education. This woman too was a great favorite among the old-timers, prisoners and officers alike. While we were there she came to visit some of her friends and was not officially invited to the reservation. A reception was arranged in her honor, in the home of one of the officers. This was one of the few occasions when I heard officers quite outspoken in their criticism of such pettiness on the part of the present Warden.

The only remnants of all these fine programs in our day was music appreciation, which I am told has since been abolished; a course on "Right Living" by the librarian Miss Aiken, who is now retired, and "Current Events" by Miss Bowman, who left to become warden of Terminal Island. The only session of her class I heard someone describe was on the life of the present British Queen Elizabeth, hardly calculated to keep the women abreast of the outside world. Betty and I avoided it. We knew, as Miss Bowman had originally said, "There is nothing here for you."

Dr. Harris does not mention the agitation created by the women political prisoners of World War I; Socialists like Kate Richards O'Hare, anarchists like Emma Goldman, who blasted the horrible conditions of federal prisoners and focused attention on the crying need of reform. Particularly effective was the activity of Mrs. Kate Richards O'Hare, one of the first to be convicted under the Espionage Act of 1917, and sentenced to five years in Missouri State Penitentiary, to which later came Emma Goldman, Mollie Steiner, and other women politicals. Mrs. O'Hare's sentence was commuted by President Wilson on evidence collected by the Church Federation of Chicago that her arrest in North Dakota, while on a speaking trip, was a frame-up. On her release she concentrated on working for amnesty for several hundred other political prisoners of World War I. She led a dramatic and effective Children's Crusade for Amnesty—"a living petition that they can't throw in the waste basket," she called it—to Washington in 1922, which caused President Harding to free their anti-war fathers, sharecroppers from Arkansas and Missouri.

After the political prisoners were released, she continued to work for prison reform, under the auspices of the Union Label League of the American Federation of Labor, in a campaign to stop prison-made goods being sold in the open market in competition with union-made. As a result of this,

Prisons' Industries was finally set up to furnish articles for prisons and federal institutions' use only. The building of Alderson too is certainly partly due to her efforts. She spoke to many organizations of women all over the country of her experiences in a prison and enlisted their support for such an undertaking.

[17]

The "Verbotens"

The Federal Reformatory for Women at Alderson, West Virginia, has tried to keep up the facade of a modern, humane institution. The natural scenery contributed to this. It was a standing joke while we were there: "What do you want? It's just like White Sulphur Springs—same air, mountains, river, trees, and flowers! You never had it so good!" The standard response was, "I want cocktails with the President, on the porch." (He had met the President of Mexico at the hotel there.) Neither officers nor inmates wore uniforms, although it was rumored they were in the offing. Visitors and lawyers remarked that they were treated more courteously than in men's prisons.

In spite of these things, there was an all pervasive atmosphere of a prison and it deepened while I was there. Little by little there was a tightening of rules, the privileges shrunk. We were far removed from the customs and spirit of Dr. Harris' days. Confidence in the women, which had brought out the best in even the worst of them, was now replaced by distrust and suspicion, an atmosphere in which the inmate was always wrong. All forms of initiative were discouraged. Suggestions were rejected, although if the administration asked the officers for proposals, for instance how to improve service in the dining room, they did not hesitate to take inmates' ideas for their own. I asked once, "Why not use larger spoons for soup instead of teaspoons?" The officer said, in all seriousness, "Yes, that would save time!"

Some of the pleasant procedures allowed by Dr. Harris but now abolished were berrypicking; invitations to honor prisoners to visit officers' homes outside the reservation on holidays; visits by inmates from one cottage to another; dances in which all participated outdoors; carols by choirsingers outside the cottages on Christmas morning, which I heard the first year I was there. It was abolished by Miss Bowman the second year. The women would say bitterly, "Anything we like becomes *verboten*." There were no organized recreational facilities except ballplaying directly in front of your own cottage.

When we first came a volunteer religious worker was there, a pleasant young woman from a Quaker college. She was allowed to go to orientation and to the cottages to visit inmates in their rooms. She treated the women as equals, was well liked and comforting. But the next year no volunteer religious worker appeared. Apparently, the procedure was abolished. It was rumored that she had been too sympathetic with the Puerto Rican nationalists to suit the authorities. She said to me of one of them: "L is a saint. Is there anything you think I can do to help her?"

In former days the inmates had farewell parties for a departing cottage-mate, serving fruit and candy from their commissary for refreshments. This was suddenly abolished. It was customary during my first year for the departing inmates to dress in their going-out clothes in the cottage. This was a source of pleasure. All would admire the clothes, hat, shoes, coat, even trying them on, expressing their delight at the changed appearance of an outgoing friend. It showed what a difference a well-fitting outfit could make. But this too was abolished. Instead, the new clothing was kept at the garment shop and the changeover made there, alone with an officer.

This caused much bitterness, since there was so little relief from monotony. A reformatory was changing rapidly into a prison.

One day we were told that hereafter we would be allowed only two plants in our room. My window sill was full with geraniums, wax begonias, and little orange and grapefruit plants I grew from seeds. I kept only the begonia, a lovely blooming plant Dorothy Rose had given to Claudia and which I had inherited. I gave away all my other plants and saw them die of neglect at the hands of others, who would forget to water them. The trend was towards austerity, stripping us of all but bare necessities. Pictures next came under the ban. Down they had to come. Cosmetics were banished from tops of bureaus, into drawers. I had several large transparent colored cards, views of French cathedrals. They were like stained glass against the light. They had come through the mail, therefore were legal. But I was warned I could not keep them, so I gave them to the priest. I was determined an inspecting officer with a greedy eye would not confiscate my church windows.

In previous times, inmates had been allowed to buy flower seeds and grow individual gardens in the yards. Some of the long termers had beautiful gardens, a joy to all. In the Spring of 1957 they were told they must give them up, as official landscaping was planned. That meant that bulldozers would destroy these little patches of beauty on which so much loving care had been lavished; watering them in dry periods, covering them over on frosty nights, taking them into the cellars in Winter. Women wept and tore their gardens up in a rage.

Some rules were so petty and mean they were positively sadistic. The women were not allowed to feed the birds, even if they bought crackers. Some enjoyed making friends with the little feathered creatures. In my room in the second cottage (of which I will write later) I had a straight chair at the writing table and an armchair by the window. I was asked in the course of my cottage mending assignments, if I could cover chairs, and would I try the one in my room. It looked very nice finished. One day soon after, I found it had been taken into the living room. A new rule had been promulgated, no armchairs in the rooms. I asked to see Miss Kinzella. Chairs seemed to be a bone of contention between us. She said I had the "privilege" of sitting in the living room. I argued that since cottage mending was my assignment I needed a comfortable chair in my room; besides I preferred to read in my own room. But it was to no avail. There were plenty of armchairs in the living room, more than enough to go around. I did not deprive anyone by having an armchair in my room instead of using it out there. Finally she made a concession. I could have another chair in my room. Big deal! I found another stiff straight-backed chair in my room. I was the oldest woman in the cottage, spent all my free time in my room, yet I never got my armchair back. Fortunately, a young Negro woman took pity on me. She said "I play cards every night. I don't need the little rocker I have in my room," so she exchanged with me. Bureaucracy such as this caused much resentment. Everyone in the cottage was annoyed and others who had armchairs feared to lose them. But fortunately, I was the only one for whom this new rule was enforced.

In earlier days if an inmate locked in sick or on the days allowed off for weekend workers she was able to go to the dining room for her meals, or given a regular tray in her room. But now all this too was changed. A lock-in was not allowed in our time to leave her room even for a shower. Breakfast for her was black coffee, with no sugar, and unbuttered toast. Lunch was bread and vegetables, but no meat. The evening "meal" was a peanut butter sandwich and a glass of milk. This sparse fare was calculated to discourage locking in. Fortunately, the few times I locked in I had my own fruit and graham crackers from commissary. However, the inmates often circumvented the restrictions by bringing any food they could safely carry away from the tables and throwing it over the transoms to the lock-ins, when the officer was elsewhere. It was a "disciplinary" but what's that between friends? There's hardly a rule the inmates could not find a way to violate; the more unreasonable the rule, the more ingenious the violation.

One Sunday a new rule forced me to lock in. For a long time I did not go to the movies. I was given a permanent release, instead of asking each time. Suddenly, there was a change, without notice. Because I had failed to indicate on the list my desire not to go, I had either to go or lock in for twenty-four hours. It got my Irish up and I locked in. Later I found the cause. A woman on the lower campus had a toothache. It was raining and she did not want to go to the movies. When she was told she could not change her mind but would have to lock in for twenty-four hours, she complained to Miss Kinzella. In the course of this discussion the whole procedure was revealed. Apparently, Miss Kinzella had not been informed by her subordinates of the existence of a general excuse and she abolished it immediately. I was the first victim of her fiat. This incident showed how futile and detrimental an appeal to a higher-up could be. Inmates were particularly fearful of appealing to Miss Kinzella, lest things be made worse instead of better by a new rule.

I really did not suffer locking in on that Sunday. The other women were so indignant, as the Sunday meals were the best, that I became a martyr to injustice. When they returned, I heard one quiet voice after another say, "Watch it, Elizabeth." The transom would fly open and meat, biscuits, cookies, ice cream, napkins, etc. came through. I had actually more than if I went to the dining room. This was their expression of protest and sympathy. Oddly enough, the officer stayed upstairs a long time that day.

Every new restriction is blamed on the inmates, even on their color and nationality. One long-time officer said to me: "It was better when we had just Americans here. Now there are too many Negroes and Puerto Ricans." Another would say, "We did better when there were fewer inmates." That one girl had wandered away during a walk or one tried to "make bush" during a dance, was considered reason enough to abolish them. Hundreds suffered years later for these isolated incidents. The monotonous routine was hard enough to bear even for those of us who had resources of reflection, reading, inquiries, discussion. But to others it was maddening. Card playing was endless. Knitting and crocheting were outlets, but yarn was expensive. There was also the aggravation that sometimes we could not buy enough at one time and later it could not be matched and we would have to wait for months to finish an article. I never knew of a place to beat Alderson for frustration. It was enough to provoke the girls to use all the four-letter words they did! Remembering my father's colorful vocabulary, it was occasionally hard for me to refrain from doing likewise.

[18]
Claudia's Departure

Claudia's sentence expired in October of 1955, ten months after we came. As the time approached, she became increasingly concerned about leaving me in Cottage 26, and urged me to try to move to another cottage. She knew from experience that life was easier elsewhere. On the other hand, I did not want to raise the issue until after she left. I was torn between anxiety to have her out of there and a feeling of desolation at losing her companionship. She developed a painful condition in her feet in September and spent 25 days in the hospital. Whether the ailment was due to working the loom with her feet or the cement floors in the craft shop or both, the doctors could not determine. I was not allowed to visit her in the hospital. The prison dictum was, "not unless there is a language difficulty, one inmate cannot visit another." I notified Mrs. Kaufman to please come at once "to discuss an urgent legal problem." She came and was able to see Claudia in the hospital. I was greatly concerned that they would keep her there until her release day, but she was returned to the cottage for a short time.

Claudia was very indignant that I had been kept in maximum security for so long. Although I did not want to give the administration satisfaction by complaining, I realized it was an outrage. If my many friends outside had known of this, they would have made strong protests. I was (and am) a leading American woman Communist. I was a political prisoner not a criminal, and a responsible adult. On the pretext of my health, I had been segregated and isolated, even within the cottage. Probably the administration expected that the women in this difficult and tragic place would give me "a bad time." I felt a grim satisfaction that so far I had managed to get along alright with maladjusted, mentally sick, retarded women, some with maniacal tempers. So far as I knew I had no enemies, and some were real friends, or as much so as can be expected in prison. Of course, it was easier with Claudia for companionship. I had explained, so no stupid conclusions could be drawn even by the most evil-minded, that we were friends and had worked together in the same office for many years. The women respected our friendship and our privacy in our conversations.

Some of their reactions to us were amusing. It was hard for them to realize we could have differences of opinion, discuss at length, yet remain the best of friends. With them, every petty difference became a major battle, and often led to violent quarrels and blows. They had no idea that our discussions were the breath of life to us and helped to keep us abreast of events in the world outside. It worried Claudia that

I did so much for other inmates. Sometimes I was exhausted at night. She felt they took advantage of me and she was correct. One day she became truly impatient with me and said, "The trouble with you, Elizabeth, is you are an idealist!" I understood what she meant, that I was not taking a scientific approach to problems there and allowing my sympathies to outweigh my judgment. A woman who overheard our conversation looked puzzled and said: "I thought it was good to be an idealist! But Claudia says it like you did wrong!" We both had to laugh, though we found it hard to explain to her.

The last period of her stay was one of further anxiety as to what would happen on her release. There was an outstanding order of deportation against her. We knew of women who had been picked up at the gate by immigration officials, and shipped to Cuba, Mexico, and other Latin American countries. Claudia was born in Trinidad, in the British West Indies. She was brought here as a small child by her parents. A representative of the British government came to see her, shortly before her sentence expired, and she requested to be allowed to go to England. Finally, Mrs. Kaufman arranged a nominal bail and for Claudia's release in her custody. This was a great relief to us, since Betty faced a similar order. I could only be sent to New Hampshire!

The night before Claudia left, a professional hairdresser, an inmate, was allowed to come from another cottage to do her hair. This was one of the few privileges allowed, especially to the Negro women. Claudia had written a number of poems, but she doubted if the prison authorities would clear them and return them to her. So she memorized every one of them and recited them all to me, while I checked her text. Then she destroyed all but one, addressed to me, which she gave me. She was letter perfect, and Mrs. Kaufman told me Claudia wrote them all out again on the train, en route home. Several were subsequently published.

Claudia gave each cottage inmate a gift which she had made —a ring, pin, ash tray, and the like. They tearfully bade her farewell at lock-up time. In the early dawn, the officer who came to dress her (this was still the procedure then) opened my door for a hurried "Goodbye." My window faced the roadway, and I was able to see her leave. She turned to wave —tall, slender, beautiful, dressed in golden brown, and then she was gone. This was the hardest day I spent in prison. I felt so alone. Betty was far away, we seldom were able to meet. I had the desolate feeling that I might never see Claudia again. When, if ever, would I get a passport? (I did finally in 1960, only to have it cancelled under the infamous McCarran Act now, while I write in 1962). A few months later, after a siege of illness in a New York hospital, Claudia was forced to go to England. Not long after that, her devoted father died. I have not seen Claudia since.

The English climate is not the best for her, but at least, under provisions of socialized medicine she is able to go to a hospital regularly for rest and treatment of her asthmatic cardiac condition. She is now the editor of a lively monthly periodical published in London, *The West Indian Gazette*. It gives news and views of the Caribbean islands, as well as of the thousands of West Indians living and working in England. It campaigns vigorously against "the colour bar," as they call discrimination and segregation, unfortunately an increasing problem. Claudia's resilient spirit and resourceful ability to adapt to all circumstances, which made her unique in Alderson, sustain her in exile. She would prefer, I know, to be in the United States, which she knows and considers her country, where she lived and worked most of her lifetime, and where she is sorely missed by her friends.

Conditions were harder for me after Claudia left. I had no one who was interested in what I read or heard from outside. If I tried to talk to other inmates their interest flagged in a short time, and they became distracted. The noise seemed intolerable. I locked in every night at seven, but the merciless radio blared until nine. My work had given out. There happened to be considerable locking up by kitchen workers and an officer asked me if I would help in the dining room. I gladly accepted. I laid out dishes, silverware, and napkins, helped serve the food and clear the tables afterwards. It was a relief to be busy.

One day one of the kitchen workers suddenly collapsed. She was serving a long sentence for bank robbery, for which her husband had divorced her and taken away her children. There was no chance of her seeing them. They lived in California. She had wanted to go to Terminal Island, but had been refused. Her mind suddenly seemed to snap. She started looking for letters in a frantic manner, appealing to me, "What did I do with them?" She had no letters. I called the officer, a strange one in our cottage, and we finally persuaded her to go upstairs and lie down. But to my amazement this officer said to me, "What did you say to her to start her off?" I sensed her antagonism to me. The other women assured her I had only the friendliest relations with the woman and when she revived she too was indignant at such a suspicion. But I smelled the foul odor of redbaiting in the air and I was not wrong. A few days later this officer, whose husband was reputed to be the mayor of Alderson, told me I need not work in the kitchen any longer. So I was back where I started.

The atmosphere in the cottage quickly changed. Inmates acted as if they were afraid to speak to me, including some I had helped a great deal, who had promised Claudia "to take care of Elizabeth," after she left. I knew something was up, but could only surmise that its source was this officer. Women in prison are easily intimidated and frightened, especially if they are struggling to regain lost days, as most of them were in Cottage 26. I did not blame them. They did not understand at first why I was suddenly under attack. I was wary as to the possibility of a frame-up, not uncommon against politicals, and felt that a stool pigeon was at work.

I should have asked to be moved. But I did not want to run away from trouble. It became evident that an addict, who was later sent to the Cincinnati workhouse, had a hand in it. She was a cottage troublemaker, and had extraordinary access to the assistant warden, Miss Bowman, running down to her office continually. The women feared her influence in the main office. One Saturday morning she was sitting in the living room and her room upstairs caught fire. It started in yarn in the box under her bed. The lid was down and the door was closed. She accused another inmate of setting the fire, but girls cleaning their rooms nearby insisted no one had entered the room. They were convinced she did it herself, to get the other girl in trouble.

I had tangled with her once. She had a habit of letting forth blood-curdling screams while playing cards. I finally asked her to stop. She retorted: "It's my penitentiary privilege. This is no old ladies' home!" She knew she had the advantage as I would not complain against another inmate. The officer who disliked me sat there but paid no attention. She was busy by the hour knitting and crocheting, for this girl. She was once heard to say, "She's the smartest one here!" She was, for their purposes.

Later, I heard she had reported to the main office that I did no work and was always talking communism to the other inmates. Several were called down and questioned as to my conversations with them. Officers too were reported to have been questioned. But I had not been interrogated. One officer told me, "Play it cool, Elizabeth," which I tried to do. Early in December, on a Saturday morning, I was told by the unfriendly officer, "You are to move today to Cottage 2 and go to work in the craft shop." It was a relief, but I wanted to find out, if I could, what had precipitated the order. I asked to see my parole officer. Fortunately, I had kept a complete record of all the work I had done since orientation. An officer had given me a notebook and suggested this, as otherwise, she said, the cottage reports would merely say, "Sewing." She said if any questions arose later, I would be able to show this work record. How wise she was! I took my book down to my parole officer who looked it over, asked to keep it for a couple of days and returned it, without comment. But apparently it settled the work issue. I did not expect her to tell me of the rumors, but I wanted the authorities to know I was aware of them.

My parole officer gave me a very plausible reason for the transfer, which I accepted, with a smile to myself. She said now that Claudia was gone and I had been there eleven months, I should be given a change. She added that up to recently Cottage 2 had been a segregated cottage and was still predominantly Negro. She felt I would have no objections to moving there and helping carry out the desegregation policy. I assured her I would be very glad to do so. So here I was, actually asked in a prison to cooperate in carrying out the law of the land as promulgated by a U.S. Supreme Court decision, which called for racial equality, which we Communists had always advocated. My crisis had passed.

When I returned to Cottage 26 after this interview, the word got around that I was leaving and the fear broke. Maybe the poor things were relieved to see me go, but they crowded around to tell me they would miss me. They helped me pack my things and carry them the two short blocks, across the campus, to Cottage 2. I left them in a friendly spirit. That they had not chimed in with the charges of one they considered a stool pigeon, took real courage and I appreciated it. Without rights, cut off from the rest of the institution, a stone's throw from seclusion, in their sad little world of misfits, they naturally felt helpless. Some timid ones did not dare speak to me on the way to work for a long time. The trouble maker was moved shortly afterwards to Cottage 9. Her room looked out on the roadway where we all passed and some were still afraid to have her see them walking or talking with me. She did not last long in that cottage, nor in another, and finally was sent back to 26. The women had her number and wherever she went she was not welcome. They gave her "a bad time!" as they say in prison.

A Change in My World

I felt I had been liberated from a prison within a prison. My new room, where I stayed for the next 18 months, was on the ground floor, facing the West, looking out on the campus. It was twice as large as the old one, with a wide window, and without bars. I could still see the hospital, Davis Hall, and Cottage 26. There were five other rooms on the corridor, with the living room at the end. Showers and toilets were directly opposite my room. It seemed much quieter, the radio was turned on low, the Negro officer who I knew greeted me politely. There seemed no tension. The room was painted a warm rose color, it had a bed, a writing table, a chest of drawers, a mirror on the wall, two chairs, one straight and the other an armchair, about which I later feuded with Miss Kinzella. The windows had ruffled white curtains, with a pink floral design. The bed had a pink Bates spread, old but serviceable. I could see beautiful sunsets over the mountains and a sky full of stars at night. The room pleased me, but I had yet to meet the residents.

The cottage could hold forty women and it was almost full. We went to the next cottage three times a day for our meals. How I enjoyed this walk in the fresh cold air, where we also met the inmates from two other cottages. When dinner time came some of the girls came to fetch me. There were as yet only a few white women there. A little Negro woman from New York told me frankly they did not really want whites there; they had a peaceful cottage and were afraid of a change. She said, "We know you are different." Some of her Bronx friends were Communists. She had once been arrested

122

in a demonstration. She took me under her wing and vouched
for me to the others. With one or two exceptions, they were
extraordinarily kind to me. They would not allow me to go
up and down the basement stairs to get my Winter coat.
They helped me in icy and snowy weather; they guaranteed
me my turn in the showers; took my laundry upstairs to turn
in for me. They waxed my floors and washed my windows;
they hardly let me do any physical labor. In return I wrote
letters, sewed for them, and gave advice.

On the following Monday I made my first trip to the arts
and crafts department which was on the other side of the
campus, about a three blocks' walk from the cottage. We took
this walk four times daily, five days a week. It was a fine
change from being cooped up in a cottage, with hardly a
break. I felt as if I knew the shop and Miss Smithson from
Claudia, but unfortunately it was her day off. A relief officer
was in charge and at a loss what to assign a newcomer. This
was but another instance of prison inefficiency. It should have
been arranged that newcomers would report on Tuesday.
However, a white-haired woman, a friend of Claudia's, came
forward and offered to find work for me to do. She brought
out a roll of beautiful place mats she had woven, which she said
she had purposely held back from the common sewing table
until she found some one who could hem them carefully. She
asked me if I would like to do them. After I did a couple, she
was satisfied. So I settled down to my new job in Alderson.

When Miss Smithson came she greeted me warmly as
"Claudia's friend Elizabeth." She told me to continue with
the place mats and I worked on them for quite a while. They
were made of what was called "Civil War linen," which was
rolled into balls. It was a natural colored thread which wove
beautifully with colored thread. The weaver worked out her
own pattern. No one knew how old the thread was or from
whence it came. Next I worked on hemming the beautiful
table cloths Claudia had woven. There were more than
thirty. They were green, yellow, blue, pink, and coral. There

was a central piece and two narrow side strips, which I joined together with tatting of the same color made by women in the shop. It was delicate work, requiring painstaking care. Miss Smithson showed me how to make mitred corners. I finished a large number for Christmas and the rest by Easter. They were used in the officers' dining room for special occasions and had to be laundered by hand.

The thread for weaving curtains, place mats, and table cloths, was brightly colored, new and clean. The rugs were made of scrap materials. Women who could not weave, for reasons of age or disabilities, cut the scraps into strips, sewed the ends together and rolled them into balls. They worked at a long table. The balls were stored in large boxes in a side room, piled one on top of the other. Another woman and I varied our sewing by going over the contents of these boxes. We found some bright red and yellow balls which made colorful rugs. Some women at the table were so inept that their work had either to be done over or discarded. Miss Smithson did not require silence, as in other prison shops, only low tones and no fighting.

The women also ripped up old nylon tow targets and parachutes from the army and navy. They had numbers on them and were enormous. They would cover the whole table and several women worked on one at the same time. Then the pieces were folded, pressed and sent to the sewing room and garment shop, to be made into underwear and nightgowns. The remnants came back to us to be used for rugs. They made such nice soft white rugs that many were taken by officers for their rooms. The inmates appreciated that we were improving on the drab rugs they were accustomed to on their floors. I urged the weavers to make them well and attractive. I said: "It may go to your cottage. The rug you weave may be your own!" Occasionally it did and they could boast of their handiwork. I suggested nothing at any time except as I saw it could benefit the inmates.

At one general clean-up we found a large quantity of

dyes in the bottom of the closet. I suggested to Miss Smithson we use it to dye the white remnants. She said it was a good idea, but she had found the dyes there when she came and had been told not to use them. Dr. Harris in her book had mentioned classes in Batik where women were taught to refresh faded cast off materials, which probably explained the dyes. But Miss Smithson could not get permission to use them and they remained stored away. We would have had a grand time dying the white cloths all colors and it would have made unusual and more practical rugs. The white ones were hard to keep clean.

Another stupid rule at the prison was that nothing could be thrown away until it was officially "condemned" by a special officer inspector. The result was that cellars and attics were full of discarded articles. Wooden shuttles used in the weave room would fall apart. They were beyond use or repair, yet we were not allowed to throw them away with the trash. They piled up in the store room, a fire hazard. Big boxes in the toilet room were also full of material unsuitable for weaving. Occasionally, we slipped a few in the incinerator. Possibly some day a congressional committee will junket to Alderson and order the dumping of tons of inflammable material, gathering dust around the place.

When I first went to the craft shop an Indian woman was in charge of the supply closet of the weaving department. When she was released Miss Smithson asked me to take charge of it. Since it only involved locking up thread and not people, I accepted the keys and had them till the day before I left. In the garment shop another "political," a Puerto Rican nationalist woman, had charge of the closet where the outgoing garments were stored, because of her unquestioned honesty. The weaving was at the back of the shop. In the front women worked in copper, silver, and leather crafts, also pottery and ceramics. The shop occupied two-thirds of the floor. The other third was used as the Catholic Chapel. This craft shop was the show place of the institution. Groups of visitors were regularly escorted through. It was actually a concentration of politicals. Two Puerto Rican patriots, an American woman charged with treason, and I, were eyed curiously by the visitors. We were not allowed to talk to them except to answer questions about the work.

"Threading" the looms was a complicated and tedious process. It required five or six women to help, since it was all done by hand. The long threads, the warp, easily became tangled and had to be handled carefully. In textile mills this is done by machinery. The only advantage I could see in our laboriously slow way of weaving was that it kept women busy on pleasant, clean and constructive work, and undoubtedly had a therapeutic value. Otherwise a return to hand labor made no appeal to me. The fabrics were not superior to machine made, and were even inferior. One girl in an orientation observation group watched the weaving and said later: "Gosh! Don't they know they can buy the stuff by the yard?"

Once a week Miss Smithson brought the current orientation group to see the craft shop. They walked all around, looked at everything, asked questions, and enjoyed a little freedom. Usually they were a sad, scared looking lot, apathetic, still stunned by finding themselves in prison. They brightened up a little in the informal shop atmosphere. Occasionally there was a returned parolee or a second timer, who would greet us as old friends and be kidded in turn: "So you like it here? You couldn't stay away! Too lazy to work! Want Uncle Sam to take care of you?" and the like.

The walls of the craft shop were adorned with drawings and paintings made by inmates. Some were excellent. There was a portrait of Congresswoman Ruth Bryan Rohde, who took a real interest in Alderson and had presented the bust of George Washington for the auditorium. There was a painting of the 64's and a copy of a self-portrait by Van Gogh, about which I wrote a poem. Miss Smithson had outdoor classes for sketching and water colors. Some of the women were quite talented. The covers for the quarterly

The Eagle were done by a woman in the shop, a painstaking process when several colors were involved. The writing and illustrations were largely done by inmates, subject to official censorship, of course.

Besides those who were assigned to work daily in the shop, others came voluntarily at night, on Saturday, and on their days off (for those who worked Saturdays and Sundays). They learned to crochet, make hook rugs, ceramics, pottery, to weave, etc. The shop workers taught them. Once a year the best of the articles were sent out to the County Fair. It was an impressive collection; dolls, toy animals, infants' wear, sweaters, purses, slippers, pottery, dishes, jewelry, woven articles. Many won prizes. The spirit in the craft shop at that time was different from any other place on the reservation. It was more like a school than a prison. The women were treated as adults. One was encouraged to show initiative even in little things to please and amuse your companions. I made heart-shaped cushions of red material for the rooms of women who had none. "By accident," I made them for all the "politicals" on Valentine's Day and for the others later.

For St. Patrick's Day I cut shamrocks out of a discarded piece of green oilcloth, enough for everybody in the shop and some extras for their cottage. My Puerto Rican friends were sceptical about St. Patrick because here was a Communist honoring a saint. They thought I made him up. But when they read a tribute to him in the weekly *Catholic Bulletin,* which the priest issued, they were surprised and convinced. My friendly relations with the priest puzzled them. They said: "You're not religious. You don't go to church. But when he comes in to the shop he talks to you!" I said: "Don't you know why? He's Irish and I am Irish!" A big light broke over their faces. "Oh, nationalism!" they exclaimed. That they understood. It was their second religion.

There was one source of irritation in relation to the shop, for which the administration was responsible. A large supply of leather briefcases were stored in the shop to be used for leather work. Undoubtedly they had been confiscated some-where. When I first came to Alderson the women were al-lowed to make moccasins in the craft shop, which they wore in the evening to rest their tired feet. Since the women were not allowed to wear their prison issued cloth house-slippers into the living room, these neat moccasins had been a god-send. Suddenly an order came through that no more moc-casins could be worn on the reservation. Either they must be put away to take out or sent home now. Leather was re-stricted to belts and purses. I saw women cry as they lost that little bit of comfort. They cursed the place in no uncertain language. The senselessness of these petty rules was a source of great aggravation.

[20]

Christmas in a Prison

I came to the craft shop as Christmas was approaching. Preparations for the holiday kept the shop in a flurry. The whole institution was busy. This was done deliberately to keep the women from lapsing into melancholy and rages of loneliness. Huge figures were designed in the shop, represent-ing Joseph, Mary with the infant Jesus in her arms, the three Kings, shepherds, angels, cows, sheep and lambs, including a black one, when it was painted. They were cut out of wood by the men carpenters of the nearby prison, were painted in our shop, and done very well. I recall the remarkably vivid eyes of Joseph, painted by a talented inmate. The images were mounted outside on a hillside, between the two levels; they were lit up by electricity and could be seen from afar. There was much hilarity, at Miss Kinzella's expense, when a stray dog found the new straw-filled empty manger and crawled in to sleep at night.

The shop also made jaunty reindeer and a fat Santa Claus for the assembly hall. They made imitation candles out of the cardboard rolls inside toilet paper rolls, candlesticks from empty thread cones, and wreaths and other decorations from evergreen branches. A large Christmas tree was set up in the shop. No presents were allowed under the tree, so they wrapped up articles from around the shop in colored paper with ribbons, including the dictionary, pottery, even the wastebasket—an ingenious and valiant attempt at celebrating Christmas. No outside gifts, except four pounds of candy from an accredited person, were allowed. This was in contrast to the treatment of politicals and other prisoners after World War I, nearly 40 years before. Emma Goldman wrote in her book *Living My Life* of her experiences in Jefferson City, Mo., state prison as follows: "Long before Christmas gifts began to arrive for me. Soon my cell began to look like a department store—bracelets, broaches, earrings, necklaces, rings—lace collars, handkerchiefs, stockings and other things, to compete with any store on 14th St. On Christmas eve, while our fellow prisoners were attending the movies, a matron accompanied me to unlock the doors, our aprons piled high with gifts. With gleeful secrecy we flitted along the tiers, visiting each cell in turn. When the women returned the cell block resounded with happy astonishment. 'Santa Claus was here! He brought me something grand too! Me too!' reechoed from cell to cell." No such gifts were allowed in Alderson.

In the 1920's when I was organizer of the Workers' Defense Union in New York, we were permitted at Christmas time to send boxes of nuts, hard candies, books, magazines, socks, underwear, and handkerchiefs to the several hundred wartime politicals still incarcerated in federal prisons. We were allowed to correspond with them, to send them money, and to have a representative of our organization, Ella Reeve

Bloor, visit them. She travelled from prison to prison. I visited a group of IWW's in Leavenworth, Communists in Sing Sing and Auburn, N.Y.; Mooney, McNamara and IWW's in California, and Joe Hill in Salt Lake City at an earlier date. All these privileges had been eliminated by the 1950's. Today contact with the outside world is at an irreducible minimum.

At Christmas in 1955 and again in 1956, Kathie sent me three round tin boxes and one square box of Barricini's chocolates. The boxes, as well as the contents, were at a premium. I sent one to the officer of Cottage 26, to be distributed among my former cottage mates. I gave one to my little friend from the Bronx in my own cottage, who received no Christmas package. I took one to the shop and kept one to treat any visitors in my room. Christmas checks came in the mail, totalling $135.00. An old friend, Miss Mary Dreier, had sent $100.00. But since she was not a regular correspondent it was impounded and I did not receive it till I came out in May 1957, a year and a half later.

On December 25, 1955, I wrote to Kathie: "I had a real present on Saturday. I was called down by my parole officer and permitted to look over my brainchild, my first book. It was a paper back and I liked it very much." These few words hardly expressed how I felt. I had written the book under great pressure during our appeal, leaving the job of editing, printing, proof-reading, even giving it a name, to others. It was called *I Speak My Own Piece*. Mrs. Kaufman had brought it with her a short time before and requested that Miss Kinzella allow me to see it. Miss Kinzella was puzzled. It was an unusual request, without precedent. Finally she agreed, because it was Christmas. So I spent a half hour savoring the joy of being an author, though I did not read it carefully until my release. My parole officer put it with my things to take out. I said if she or any others cared to read it, they were welcome. I suspect a few did.

But try as we would, Christmas was a bad time in prison.

Everyone longed for home and freedom. We envied those officers who were with their families. The choir prepared a good musical program for the church services and the priest and minister did their best to preach cheerful sermons, to comfort and console. But many tears were shed and even an extra-special dinner did not make up for the separation from those we held dear. A few long-timers were allowed to talk to their families by 'phone, but here too tears at both ends usually drowned out all attempts at conversation.

My correspondents sent a lot of fancy cards for the holidays for me to distribute. I had enough Santas to decorate the doors of all the women in my cottage and to take some to the shop. I had some wreath-like ones which women put in their windows. One of my cards of the Nativity was so simple and appealing, that an artistic girl copied it on a window of her cottage. Another was a folding one of angels, singing as a choir. My little Bronx friend, who was on the paint crew, took it to show to them. They were so delighted with it, they wanted to give it to their officer, who was a great favorite. They offered to pay for it, to buy me a commissary. I sent back word they could keep it—free, of course. Each wrote their name on one of the figures. A number of cards came after Christmas, which I saved for the next year.

I should add that in relation to the Jewish holidays, it was claimed that there were not enough Jewish women there to warrant the presence of a Rabbi. For their holidays, Miss Smithson, the dietitian, sister of Miss Smithson of the craft shop, secured matzohs for them, the priest furnished candles, and one of the inmates read the appropriate rituals. It was true there were very few Jewish women in Alderson. This is credited in part to the special concern of Jewish women's organizations for juvenile delinquents of their faith.

Christmas would be much more endurable if prisoners were allowed to exchange gifts; many actually do in spite of the prohibition. Dr. Harris had encouraged generosity. But it was discouraged by the present administration. There were rumors of disciplinaries one Christmas. It was a relief when the Christmas holiday came to an end and all signs of it disappeared. New Year's assumed a different aspect, of time passing. Old calendars were thrown away. The priest gave out new ones. Days, weeks, months, years, were re-counted, awaiting the longed for release. I faced my second year with far more equanimity. I was used to the place now, and liked the craft shop as much as one can like anything in a hated existence. Kathie sent me the monthly *Sky Reporter* from the Hayden Planetarium in New York. I resubscribed for my paper and magazines, had an annual anti-tetanus shot and prepared to keep myself as busy as possible. My schedule now included, in addition to my eight-hour day in the shop, two hours a week in sewing class, two hours in music appreciation, as well as my library period. I had been dropped in the Fall from the music period because Betty and I talked in class. I was finally reinstated. But I missed Betty Gannett. It had been our only opportunity to exchange news.

The news was interesting by now. The U.S. Supreme Court had accepted the appeal of Oleta Yates, who had a five-year contempt sentence added to her five-year Smith Act sentence, in California. The Court had also agreed to review the California and Pennsylvania Smith Act cases, which was a real break for all such appeals. When Kathie came for her January–February visit she brought her daughter with her, which was a great joy for me. Time passed and I began to see real meaning in the marker with an arrow on the corner outside my window which pointed to "Exit."

But I was disturbed to find my weight had increased since I came to the new cottage. The change, the Christmas goodies, more outdoor life, all contributed. I decided I must again take myself in hand. I had already lost fifty pounds and did not intend to take it on again. I decided my 1956 resolution must be to cut out starches, fats, sweets, pastries. (Would that I had the will power outside I had in there!) As I wrote to Kathie, "I am mending my way (not ways) through Alderson." Little things marked my weight reduction. I wrote another time, "The corselette I wore in is now wore out!" I was able to order a smaller one, a comfort at least. It took three months before I received it.

The center of my activities was now the shop, not the cottage, which was a place to sleep, eat, read. But I did not become involved in the problems of the cottage inmates as I had done in No. 26. They were much more self-sufficient and did not expect it, which was a relief to me. I tried not to get involved in problems of shopmates, either, to too great an extent. It was a physical and emotional strain. Claudia had been right about this. But I wrote letters, as usual, to all official bodies, for inmates.

One girl had an eye infection and had started a very abusive letter asking to be released from farm work. The whistle blew and she had to rush out of the cottage to be picked up by the truck. She threw it on the table and said: "Please Elizabeth, finish it for me!" I read it and realized it would get her nowhere.

I added to her letter: "I know I should not be so angry and impatient and am sure you will excuse it when you realize how I suffer from my eye. And I am so worried that I will lose my sight. I believe it is re-infected from the soil. So please change my job. I don't mind hard work. I'd be willing to go on the paint crew—anything to let my eye get better." I gave the note to the officer who sent it through channels. The inmate was amazed and delighted when she got her reassignment to the paint crew. She said, "Elizabeth, I don't understand it, after I blew them away, the way I did!" I told her, "Well, I used a little diplomacy after that!"

Women in the Craft Shop

The women who worked in the shop came from both campuses. We got all the prison news. One came from Betty's cottage and at long last we were able to communicate with each other. Many subscribed to their hometown papers and I saw Pittsburgh and Denver papers while Smith Act trials were going on there. When they knew my interests, women brought me clippings about Communist trials or personalities wherever the word appeared in a paper. I had a private clipping service. They brought me pictures of Steve Nelson on trial in Pittsburgh, from many papers. After Claudia left women who received the Negro periodicals, *Ebony* and *Jet,* loaned them to me. White women were not allowed to subscribe to Negro periodicals. Finally, *Jet* was barred as too sensational. A few read the Negro press and I saw copies of the (Baltimore) *Afro-American,* the (Pittsburgh) *Courier,* the (Chicago) *Defender,* and the (New York) *Amsterdam News.* I read of the release of my friend Benjamin J. Davis and of his subsequent marriage. I also read of the recovery of Paul Robeson from a major operation—news *The New York Times* did not see fit to print.

Sitting at the table sewing I heard many stories, pathetic, humorous, fantastic. Most of those in the weave shop were "short-termers," involved in lesser offenses; making moonshine, small tax evasion, contempt of court, checkpassing, and the like. At the table were mostly older women, heavy, sick, crippled, some retarded. There were cardiacs, diabetics, paralytics, arthritics, rheumatics, neurotics, and a couple of bored adolescents. The long-termers were in the craft shop, some narcotic addicts. Not too many were pleasant companions. They were irritable, quick to imagine insults and grievances, fault finding, trying to take advantage of each other. It was hard to tell what was true or false in their tales.

Some cases had been publicized so much that these poor women seemed to be in a goldfish bowl. Such was the situation of Mrs. Cora Shannon, who was not well enough to work and came to the shop to make pottery gifts for her grandchildren. She and her daughter, the widow of "Machine-Gun Kelly" who died in Leavenworth Penitentiary, had life sentences for kidnapping. They had been there over 25 years. Her account of the changes in the place interested me and confirmed my judgment that she had seen it transformed from an industrial institution into a prison that was steadily becoming worse, not better. She wore a sunbonnet, a relic of earlier days at Alderson. She made fine handkerchiefs and sweaters, which she sold to pay for her pottery materials. She was the only inmate there who was universally called Mrs. It was respect for her age. All attempts by these two women to secure parole were checkmated by the vindictiveness of the kidnap victim, a wealthy businessman, and his relatives, although he had not been harmed. The women were considered accessories because they were at the farmhouse where he had been kept. Both of them were recently released by a long overdue court order.

There was another mother-daughter pair in the shop. The daughter was a grandmother. They were in for "moonshine" in a Southern state. They were hard-working farmwomen from a remote area. The older one was a dictatorial matriarch, obviously responsible for the setup which sent her whole family to prison. But she blamed her husband and son-in-law for the plight, though she hoped to get out first so she could order them around again.

There were several mother-daughter teams in Alderson. One pair were in our cottage and their husbands were also in prison for moonshine. The daughter had left a small baby outside. Her "crime" was that she dropped the jug and so destroyed the evidence against her mother. One day as I was going home from work, the friendly young doctor who came from Brooklyn, told me: "Well, today we have three generations in Alderson." A mother-daughter team lived in another cottage, and the daughter had a baby girl born that day. Neither the inmates nor officers, especially the Southerners, considered "moonshine" a crime. They treated these simple backwoodsy women with sympathy and indulgence. They made parole sooner than others. A parole board member asked one, "Did you make good stuff?" The old lady retorted: "I sure did! Come down and try it!"

One older white woman from the far South had been called before a grand jury investigating a ring of white slavers, who were accused of bringing girls into the United States from Latin America. She refused to answer all questions and was sentenced to a year for contempt of court. She raged incessantly at the injustice of it. She had spent a fortune for lawyers, only to be in a prison. She was very cagey about her affairs, though some inmates who knew her said she had a string of "houses." One day I asked her: "If you had answered those questions, would you have been in trouble yourself? Would you have done what the lawyers call incriminate yourself?" She looked at me suspiciously and said, "Sure, I'd have been in real trouble." I said, "Well, in that case, you could have taken the 5th Amendment." She had never heard of it, so I explained carefully. "My God!" she exploded. "I pay those s.o.b. lawyers to defend me and a Communist woman in prison has to tell me my rights." Everybody laughed but she mumbled and growled till her lawyer came. She shouted her angry protest at him. "Where did you hear about the 5th Amendment?" he demanded. "A Communist woman told me!" she shouted. "She would," he said in disgust.

This woman told the most incredible tale I heard in Alderson. She said a girl friend of hers had an affair with a rich man. Finally he broke it off and left for Europe with his wife. The deserted sweetheart was indignant that all he left her was a pair of long gloves, which she threw away. Months later the woman who told me the story met the man and upbraided him: "Why did you leave my friend such a cheap present, a pair of gloves?" He answered: "Didn't she try them on? There was a $1000-bill stuck in each finger!" The cries of horror from around the table was something to hear. Maybe she made it all up but her story held the listeners rapt. I'll bet no one there will now ever throw away a new pair of gift gloves without a search.

A tragic figure was led into the craft shop one day by a girl from her cottage, who came later to take her back. She was frightened and numb-looking, bedraggled, with her hair in long frowsy braids. She was an Indian girl from a reservation, who had killed her mother and received a life sentence. She had not spoken a word since she came to Alderson. At first she just sat there. Miss Smithson sat with her, talked to her low and gently, and finally persuaded her to do some work on leather. Finally, one day she spoke. Later she smiled. It was as if we had seen a miracle. As weeks passed she finally came alone to the shop, with a neat dress and her hair combed. She answered shyly in monosyllables if we spoke to her. No one asked her story. She was like one returned from the dead.

I was especially sorry for a young Negro girl, less than twenty. She seemed like a child, yet was so old and horribly corrupt in all the ways of prison. She had spent most of her short life in institutions, had lived in practically all the cottages and was now in No. 26. She had tried every occupation on the reservation and wilfully failed at all of them. She pleaded to get out of Cottage 26 part time at least, so she was assigned to the craft shop, to the horror of women there who knew her. They protested to Miss Smithson that she was a troublemaker and her language was the worst on the reservation. She came in rather meekly and Miss Smithson took her into the kiln room for a private talk. She said: "I will not let you stay here unless you talk clean. The women here are all nice women. Nobody here like's dirty talk." The girl promised and to everyone's surprise, except for one or two slips of the tongue, which we ignored, she kept her word faithfully till the day of her release. It wasn't easy for her.

Of course, she had a language of her own. One of her favorite expressions was "Dig man!" Once I asked her, "Will you teach me that language?" She was vastly amused and told everyone, "Elizabeth wants to be hep to dig man talk." Hers was a combination of prison, junkie, jive and teenage jargon. To her I was a "square," one who knew nothing of "the life" or the criminal world. Anything she liked was "crazy." To leave the prison was "splitting." To be free was "on the street," never to go home. Money was "bread," a "cat" was a fellow who was not a square; "dig" was to understand. I cannot begin to recall all the weird expressions this child used. Some were inoffensive sounding but had vile double meanings. She would say of this: "Don't ever say that. It means more than you know." If I as much as said damn or hell, she and others would rebuke me. "What will your friends think when you go home?"

She had a good mind, had finished the prison high school course and had her diploma. She developed original designs for weaving when she was so inclined. She told me bits of her story. While a very little girl she and a white child companion had been raped. She had a terrible fear of men as a consequence, and would not allow one to come near her. Women officers, not guards, took her to seclusion. She was afraid to be out after dark. She screamed wildly if a male doctor approached her in the hospital and the women nurses had to examine her. She was apparently irrecuperable and was notorious as a lesbian on the reservation.

Her clothes were a mess, shoes rundown, no socks, torn slacks. But as the going-out time approached for us (she and I left the same day), she became interested and impressed with the nice little blue suit made for her in the garment shop. We went down together to try on our outfits. She looked at me in a blue dress and at herself in the mirror and said, "Boy! We sure look different." She was fearful that she was not being released but would be sent to another institution until she was 21. No one who knew would tell her. I do not know what happened. She left before I did. As I signed the book for my money and effects, I noticed the line ahead. She had signed for exactly one penny!

In the craft shop one of the weavers was a young blonde, about 25 years of age—gentle, soft spoken—a narcotic addict. Her husband had been released from prison shortly before her release. She showed us his picture; dark-haired, handsome, smiling. He wrote he would be waiting. He stayed at White Sulphur Springs. Her mother wrote pleading with her to come home, desperately reminding her that she had been in trouble ever since she met Harry. We all urged her to go home. She was in a quandary and very unhappy. She had been caught up in a vicious circle of drugs, romance, high life. She was a good weaver, had a sense of colors, read good books. She kept saying, to try to build up her resistance: "I want to go straight. I don't want any more prison." Before she left she came in with a sprig of flowers which she stuck in my hair and thanked me for being so good to her. Then she was gone and we heard no more of her.

But a few months after I came home I saw a newspaper account of their arrest in England. Her husband was accused of stealing $37,000-worth of jewelry at the Hotel Savoy Plaza in New York City. She was charged with receiving stolen goods. On their return, under guard, their pictures showed a smiling well-dressed young couple, waving like movie stars. She had jeweled earrings and a mink stole. He told the police that narcotics cost them $35 a day and they had planned to stay in England, where addicts can register and get narcotics on a doctor's prescription, at a nominal rate. He received a light sentence after making complete restitution. But he committed another robbery and this time got a heavy sentence to Auburn Prison. She was left alone, penniless and friendless, either rejected by her family or ashamed to go home. On July 5, 1959, she took an overdose of barbiturates and was found dead in a hotel room, at 28 years of age. She had been arrested eleven times on narcotic charges; her husband had been arrested ten times since they met in 1954.

If there is a moral to the tragic story of this poor girl who loved not wisely but too well, it is that addicts are sick people. They are driven to crime by the prohibitive cost of drugs. Prison does not cure the habit. Gangsters prey on addicts and make millions. She was a victim. She took the easiest way.

[22]

The Politicals in Alderson

On one of my visits to the clinic, while Claudia was still in Alderson, I saw a stout little white-haired woman, who spoke with a Spanish accent. She smiled and smiled at me with such cordiality that I felt she must be someone special. When I described her to Claudia she said, "That's Blanca, one of the Puerto Rican nationalists." I had often heard Claudia speak of this woman, whose beautiful face resembled Dolores Ibarruri of Spain, known as La Pasionaria. Claudia wrote a poem in tribute to Blanca called "My Anti-Fascist Friend." One of the first to greet me on my arrival at the craft shop was this woman, Blanca Torresola, as she was known in the prison, although her family name in the formal Spanish style of Puerto Rico is Blanca Canales Torresola. Like us, she was a political prisoner, serving a five-year sentence.

In her country she was a well-known social worker, who

belonged to a leading family. I heard that her brother was a member of the Puerto Rican House of Representatives. She had been a member of the revolutionary Nationalist Party and a great admirer of their revered leader, Dr. Pedro Albizu Campos, who is now in prison for life, in his country. When I told her I had visited him years ago in the Columbus Hospital in New York, her eyes sparkled with excitement. A woman who knows her at home told me she was one of the best-dressed women there, had her own car, and was extremely competent. Later, when I knew Blanca better, I told her this. She laughed merrily and said, "My friends should see me now!" She had never been in the United States before coming to prison and she suffered a great deal from the cold in Winter. She wore blue slacks and tied them at the ankles over heavy socks. She wore a heavy overcoat, much too large for her, which came to her shoe tops, and a knitted stocking cap with a muffler. But even in this quaint attire there was a certain dash to this little woman.

Her sentence expired in December 1956. She was then taken under guard to Puerto Rico, to the Escuela Industrial de Mujeres (Industrial School for Women) at Vega Alta to serve a life sentence. As far as I know, she is still there. Her two sentences arose out of the turbulent period in 1950 when uprisings occurred. The Nationalist Party protested against commonwealth status and demanded complete independence from the United States for Puerto Rico. When I asked her what caused her arrest she replied they had seized the post office in her home town and hoisted the Nationalist flag over it. Apparently there was no resistance. Possibly this explained why she had two sentences, if the post office was U.S. property. But the life sentence, for revolutionary activity, was ferocious.

She worked on a small hand loom. She had a heart condition and was neither strong nor tall enough to operate a wide loom. But she was one of the best weavers and taught others. She made place mats in lovely contrasting colors. She helped those who had weaving difficulties. She was a devout Catholic and wove altar cloths for the chapel. Although we differed on politics and religion, we were able to discuss and disagree in a friendly manner. It was a pleasure to discuss a wide range of topics with such an intelligent woman; current affairs, books, music, social problems, prisons, and the like. Claudia was happy to hear that Blanca and I had become friends.

She had a lively sense of humor. One day she told me she did not feel well and would lock in after lunch. But she returned, and told me that their fussy old lady officer had suddenly ordered the Puerto Rican women to "Speak English, so I can understand you!" Blanca mobilized those who were in the cottage to stand outside, and led them in singing the Puerto Rican freedom hymn. The officer heard the hub-bub and rushed to the door. Immediately retracting her silly order she said, "Come in for your lunch and speak all the Spanish you like!" Blanca said, laughing triumphantly, "How could I lock in for sick, when I made all that big noise and exercise?" Although there has been amnesty for many politicals in Puerto Rico this elderly woman, who has heart trouble and arthritis has met with no mercy there.

There were three other Puerto Rican nationalist women in Alderson. Carmen Torresola, a young woman, was the widow of Guisello Torresola, a relative of Blanca's who was killed in 1950 by a guard at a nationalist demonstration in Washington, D.C. Her young children were with her family in Puerto Rico. On her release she returned there and remarried. Another was a tall stately woman, Rosa Collazo, wife of Oscar Collazo, who is serving a life sentence in Leavenworth prison, charged with shooting a guard in Washington, D.C., in one of their demonstrations. Neither of these women had been in Washington nor had they participated in either demonstration; but they were charged with conspiracy under the "acts of violence" section of the Smith Act. They were sentenced to four and six years respectively. They had both been garment workers in New York and were assigned to the garment shop in Alderson. They came regularly to the craft shop. I also saw Carmen in the sewing class, where she made lovely little dresses for her children.

We had become acquainted with Carmen and Rosa in the New York House of Detention. There was a third Puerto Rican nationalist there but on another floor, so we did not meet her. Shortly after I came to the weave shop in Alderson, she was assigned there. Lolita Lebrun was a tiny little woman, sentenced to from eight to 50 years, virtually for life. She looked childlike, although she had a daughter 16 years old, who was married and had a baby. It seemed fantastic that Lolita, with her hair down her back in a braid tied with a ribbon, could be a grandmother! Blanca had not known her but was naturally delighted to see her. She took her under her wing, taught her all she knew about weaving until Lolita became an expert, weaving beautiful curtains. They talked all day in Spanish, in a very animated manner, and appeared to be happy together.

But Lolita was usually very sad, seldom smiled and talked very little except to Blanca. Her young son had been killed in a car accident during her trial; her brother had turned state's evidence against her and her comrades; her aged mother did not know she was in prison. She had been a garment worker in New York and the family tried to keep up this pretense to the mother. I tried once to say it was too bad they had gone with guns to shoot up Congress in Washington, that a big banner with the words "Freedom for Puerto Rico" would have been much more effective. The American people would have understood that and their sentences would probably have been just for disorderly conduct. But she explained passionately: "I expected to die! I am ready to give my life for my country!" I soon realized that religion and politics were two subjects which excited her too much. We all refrained from them; she had enough to bear.

She worked in the shop from February to December 1956. She became more and more reserved, talking to no one, finally hardly to Blanca. She prayed constantly. While we rested during a smoke period she went into the toilet room, knelt on the concrete floor to pray among the mops and brooms. When a girl put a pillow there for her, she rejected it. Her knees were calloused. We asked if she could be permitted to go into the Catholic chapel to pray, the door was wide open. But the head office refused permission. She had an improvised altar in her room, where she prayed at night. When she went to confession the women said she sobbed uncontrollably. But she offended no one, did her work diligently, was gentle and kind, never complained. Everyone felt sorry for her. Her sorrow, plus her terrible sentence, undoubtedly caused her to take refuge in religion. It was a solace to her.

One day a call came from the hospital for Lolita to come there. We thought nothing of it as a number of women from her cottage were ill from food poisoning. We presumed it was a routine check. When she did not return we thought they had kept her in the hospital, with the others. But as we left the shop the "grape vine" began to work. A girl passing told us: "They took Lolita back to her cottage and are sending her to St. Elizabeth's tonight. They say she's crazy." This had come out of a clear sky, a sneak attack, as was so common in Alderson. Miss Smithson had not been apprised of it. I found out that the priest had not been consulted. Who decided, was the important question. There were no psychiatrists or experts in mental diseases there. If it could happen to Lolita in the twinkling of an eye, it could happen to any political prisoner there. I was greatly disturbed and decided to see the priest, after hearing an officer say, "She is suffering from religious mania." Many of the officers were Protestant and anti-Catholic. I said to the priest: "I'm sure you are concerned about Lolita as a Catholic. I am concerned about her as a political prisoner. I am not religious as you know, but who has a right to say she is insane because she prays a great deal?" Nothing could be done, except that he was able to call the priest at St. Elizabeth's and ask him to look after

her. "For observation," was the explanation given him in response to his inquiries. It brought home to me how helplessly
at the mercy of the prison authorities we all were.

Later I read of the release of Ezra Pound, charged with
treason but never tried, on the basis of mental incompetency.
He had been kept at St. Elizabeth's in his own private quarters, enjoying many privileges. Humanitarian poets, prom-
inent writers, and others, finally secured his release and he
was allowed to go to Italy. Being subjected to the strain of
association in the hospital with the many types of mentally
ill women who were there, was a horrible punishment for a
sensitive high-strung woman like Lolita. Actually, all she had
done was to wave a flag and shout, "Freedom for Puerto
Rico!" I have heard that she was returned to Alderson prison
in December 1958, and is now assigned to making hats for
outgoing inmates. My heart goes out to this poor little
woman, and I hope my words move some humanitarian men
and women in our country to help secure her release and let
her return to her native land. She will have served eight
years by January 1963.

The other woman whom we considered a political and who
was certainly discriminated against, as we were, was Mildred
E. Gillars, commonly known in the press as "Axis Sally," an
American woman convicted of treason in 1949 for broadcasting for the Nazis during the war. She was sentenced to from
10 to 30 years. We first heard of her when the U.S. marshals
escorting us to prison said, "You'll see Tokyo Rose and Axis
Sally there!" Later I suppose they said, "You'll see Gurley
Flynn and the other Communist women leaders there!" This
tends to incite newcomers against women already there. Marshals should be ordered not to discuss the prison inmates, as
if they were a circus parade. At first I saw her going daily to
the photography room, where she developed all pictures
taken of inmates, officers, guards, and others. I was not inclined to be sympathetic, but Claudia, who worked with her
in the craft shop, said, "Don't judge her until you hear her

story," which was always good advice in prison. She smiled and spoke pleasantly, but only to those who spoke to her first. She was an expert in all the crafts and taught Claudia to weave.

I realized that this woman was under a pitiless searchlight of constant publicity and gossip, in and out of the prison, even after seven years. Inmates would whisper: "You know what she did? Made lampshades out of the skins of our soldiers!" I reacted with horror and showed them in the *World Almanac* that the charge against her was broadcasting and that the woman they were talking about was Ilse Koch, the German woman, who was sentenced to life in 1951 for such deeds, after inciting the murder of Buchenwald prisoners. I wondered if she was still in prison. Mildred had no money but she sold her beautiful woven articles, made on a loom in her cottage, to officers, visitors, and inmates; also, she sold ceramics, earrings, and leather goods. Everything she made was in great demand, orders even coming from Washington. She was in charge of the kiln in the shop, an exacting job, packing and unpacking the work of many women. She cleaned and regulated the kiln and was scrupulously fair in the firing job, playing no favorites. But no matter how much she did in photographing, in the shop or in her cottage, she was never given a single day of meritorious or industrial time. Nor did she get a vacation in ten years from the monotonous round of 6 AM to 9 PM.

After talking to this woman for many months I became convinced Claudia was right when she said: "Mildred is no Nazi. Try to get her story." She was what I would call apolitical, knowing very little of politics. Her interests were art, music, literature, and the theatre. She had lived in Germany for 18 years. She had been in love with a German professor, Otto Koishevitz, who taught at Hunter College in New York. After his death she was alone in Germany. She needed the job she secured at the radio station. If she had quit after Pearl Harbor or renounced her American citizenship while broadcasting, as Professor Sittler of Queens did, she would be in the clear as he is today.

She was arrested by the Americans in Germany in 1946. She was held in prison there for two years, the only American woman among the German war criminals of all descriptions. A soldier accompanied her to the toilet. She did not have a change of underwear. A U.S. government man came to interrogate her and, shocked at her state, he recommended that she be transferred. There was something about her being released at one time by the American authorities and then re-arrested, but I did not get the details clearly. She was held in jail in Washington, D.C. She had no friends here, no money, no lawyer, only a half-sister who hardly knew her, but tried to help. She came to trial in 1949 with a court-appointed lawyer, who made a perfunctory defense. One of her prosecutors, T. L. Caudle from St. Louis, has since been ousted as Assistant Attorney-General, under accusations of bribery and other fraudulent dealings.

Drew Pearson is quoted as saying there were no witnesses against her until he drummed up some. One ex-soldier I met lately, who heard her, could remember only that she played fine music on her program. He said the soldiers called her Berlin Mary, that "Axis Sally" was a name pinned on her by the U.S. press here. It was enough to convict her after the war. The principal witness against her was the German head of the radio station, who was working for the U.S. Army at the time of her trial.

She made some deep blue steins for her half-sister. One had a motto in German from Goethe, "Accept your fate for it is sealed." I said, "Surely you do not believe that, Mildred?" I tried to persuade her there is always hope. But even when the time came when she could apply for parole she waived it. She was painfully fearful of publicity.

I showed her news of similar cases. Constance Drexel, a Philadelphia socialite was held on the same charge but never brought to trial. I told her of Ezra Pound who was then held without trial in St. Elizabeth's. I called her attention to cases of German war criminals who were being released. One, Joachim Peiper, Commander of the Nazi Elite Guardsmen, had been found guilty of responsibility for the Malamedy forest massacre of Christmas 1944, when 142 Americans were killed. His sentence of 35 years was commuted in December 1956. He had served less than one-third of it. This was by order of the Parole and Clemency Board of six—American, British, French, and West German. Reading all this, I could not be enthusiastic about keeping this woman in prison.

She finally did apply for parole at the end of 12 years and was released in July 1961. She was over 60 and the newspapers said she sought seclusion in a convent where she would teach. So ended the story of the talented girl born in Maine, who went to Dresden to study for a stage career during the depression years and to be near a German professor who never married her.

Before we came to Alderson there had been other politicals there. One, Helen Bryant, secretary of the Anti-Fascist Refugee Committee, had written a book about Alderson called *Inside*. Four other women members of that committee received short sentences, three for contempt of court, because they had refused to divulge to the House Un-American Activities Committee names of contributors and of the Spanish prisoners to whom aid was sent. Recently a pacifist woman from Philadelphia, who participated in demonstrations at an army site, served a short sentence there. A trade union woman from Cleveland, Marie Haug, convicted of conspiracy under the Taft-Hartley law, has just served 18 months in Alderson. So my ardent hope to be the last political prisoner sent there was not fulfilled.

23

To Disciplinary Court

While in Alderson I bought yarn at the commissary for at least five women who needed sweaters. If they could not knit themselves, it was the custom at Alderson among the prisoners to give the inmate who would knit the sweater an equivalent amount of yarn. For one who did not knit I was a heavy purchaser of yarn and nothing was said at the commissary about it. However, the last year I was there I landed in the disciplinary court over one of the hidden rules. A slight Negro woman, who lived next door to me in Cottage 2, suffered from epilepsy. She worked on a maintenance crew, going from one cottage to another to clean. She suffered from the cold so I offered to buy yarn, if she could get somebody to make her a sweater. She found an orientation sister of hers in another cottage who agreed to do it, without charging her the extra yarn. It was a nice sweater, well made, and her friend left it with a friendly officer for the maintenance worker to pick up on her next round.

Unfortunately, the officer who knew the deal went off shift. A cantankerous old lady, widow of a prison guard, the one who had tangled with Blanca, came on. She adhered to every rule she ever knew or heard of and the inmates dreaded to see her. She demanded to know to whom the sweater belonged, and unearthed enough information to send it to Control, for investigation. In a day or two I heard that they were interrogating girls in that cottage as to who bought the yarn. I would not allow someone else to be blamed and possibly lose time for what I had done. So I wrote a note to Miss Bowman, to the surprise of my officer, telling her I had bought the yarn for my needy neighbor. All three of us were called to Disciplinary Court, which consisted of Miss Bowman, my parole officer, and another officer. The other two women were too frightened to talk, so I made the argument. None of us denied our part in the transaction. It was a deed of kindness and no recompense was involved. I said, "If it's a rule that no one can give yarn to another, why do you sell it to women who cannot knit?" I got no answer, but I knew it. Yarn was one of the most profitable commodities sold there.

It was common knowledge that dozens of skeins changed hands in deals. Under these conditions a sweater cost more in there than to buy one outside. I argued that if the women were told in advance that they could bring sweaters in, making them here would not be at such a premium. Miss Bowman interrupted me to say, "This is not a resort." But I reminded her that, thanks to the advice I had received outside, from Mrs. Frankfeld, I had two sweaters while this poor woman had none. She asked the woman, "Haven't you been furnished with warm underwear?" The woman replied, "No." It was promised there and then. But to the day she left she never received it.

Miss Bowman then asked, "When you were in orientation did you not hear a rule read that gifts from one inmate to another are forbidden?" The other women both answered "Yes," but before I could reply my parole officer spoke up. She said: "When Elizabeth was in orientation there was no such rule, Miss Bowman. You made it after you became assistant warden." The court was at an impasse. With a frosty smile Miss Bowman said, "Well don't let it happen again!" and the sweater was confiscated. My poor little neighbor cried all the way home, but within the next few days she received at least three sweaters, an expression of protest and sympathy from other inmates. The new sweater was brought to the craft shop by an officer from Control to be ripped up. But Miss Smithson said indignantly, "I'm certainly not asking Elizabeth to do that," and she threw it on a top shelf in the kiln room. When my neighbor went home she was allowed by the cottage officer to take all the gift sweaters with her.

This "no gifts" rule was honored more in the breach than in observance. In fact, it was universally ignored. On Christmas and holidays, in spite of admonitions, there were gifts. Presents were given to departing inmates. Shortly after my session at the disciplinary court, a Southern Negro woman who had worked in the hospital and was very kind to all, prepared to go home. The inmates called me to see how her bed was covered with gifts. They laughed and said, "And you nearly went to seclusion over a measly sweater!" The officer checked her out without question or comment. But I began to worry about some nice things Claudia had given me, all of which she had made; two ash trays, a small pitcher, a flower bowl, a handwoven towel. I bundled them up and arranged for Kathie to take them home, lest some officious officer would challenge them under the "new rule" as gifts, and I might lose them.

But when something really vicious happened the authorities usually completely failed to catch up with the culprits. Such was the case of a nurse from the Midwest—"a den mother" of Cub Scouts, she boasted—who offered to make socks, sweaters, and mufflers for others, if they gave her yarn to make things for her grandchildren. She had at least a dozen ready customers and she stalled all of them until the day of her departure arrived. She pretended she was afraid of getting into trouble and losing time, after what happened with me. She promised to leave all the articles with the librarian aide, to be picked up on Saturday morning after she left. But when they came the bewildered girl at the desk had nothing for them and knew nothing of the affair. Women who had arranged with her to make things for their children and grandchildren, cried with disappointment. Apparently, she had used all the yarn for her own purposes and there had been no check on where she got so much yarn. If there had been they would have discovered she purchased very little. But it showed how easily petty thievery and chicanery can occur and there is no protection for the victims in a prison.

The only other instance I know of a political prisoner taken before a disciplinary court was much more serious than my experience. While a sister visited Mrs. Regina Frankfeld, one of the Baltimore Smith Act victims, the little daughter became restless and querulous. The sister had an innocuous letter of greetings. She nervously thrust it into Mrs. Frankfeld's hand and said, "Here you read it yourself." When the visit was over Mrs. Frankfeld was taken directly to seclusion and her sister was arrested in New York. They were brought before a federal court in West Virginia but the judge did not take as serious a view as the Alderson administration, and dismissed the charge of illegally passing and receiving contraband material. Mrs. Frankfeld lost days, however, sufficient to delay her departure for two months. I used to tell Kathie, "Put your coat and purse on a chair far away from me and do not open it near me or show me anything." I have heard officers caution families not to show pictures or letters to inmates. Where no harm was done common sense would dictate not to make a big issue of a mistake. But common sense was a minus quantity in a prison. There was always the danger that anything connected with "politicals" would be blown up to monstrous proportions.

24

Banished from Alderson

I do not know on what basis it was decided that women federal prisoners be sent to Alderson. Some went to federal hospitals; some to local and state institutions. It could not be based on the length of sentence because women with sentences of a few months have been sent to Alderson. It was a puzzle.

One way the Federal Reformatory for Women has tried to keep up its pretense as a model institution, it appears, was to ship its incorrigibles and their problems elsewhere. Some went to St. Elizabeth, some to the Cincinnati Workhouse in Ohio, apparently the "Alcatraz" in the field of women's prisons. Some are sent to a comparable Southern institution. The exiling of a large group from Alderson a few years before we came was legend. They made moonshine, broke down a door, and attempted to flee in an officer's car.

From all descriptions Alderson was far better than the Cincinnati jail, which was an old fashioned cellblock structure, with tier on tier of iron cells. Yet, oddly enough, some women preferred Cincinnati to Alderson. To them the mountains were oppressive, nature meant nothing, the night silence was weird. They would say: "You know you're in jail there. It doesn't pretend to be a goddam boarding school! It's in the city, not out in the wilderness. You can hear the city. You don't have to work, like here. People can come to see you a lot easier.

One of the banished was an enormously fat white woman, with an infantile mind, the one my friend A had threatened with the scissors in Cottage 26. She was there for extortion, attempting to extract money from a grief-stricken family by claiming to know the whereabouts of their kidnapped child. It was a fraud; fortunately for her she knew nothing. The actual kidnappers were caught and executed for killing the child. Her favorite prison pastime was removing locks and throwing them out the window. Once she took all the locks from the doors and windows of Cottage 26 living room, a pleasant room, with a locker full of books, a toilet and washroom. It looked out on Davis Hall and the hospital and the girls talked out the windows to passersby. When an officer discovered the loss of the locks, the room was closed. It remained so for a long time until strong screens were put up. The culprit went to seclusion. Next she stopped up all the cottage plumbing. The guards came and probed and pumped until the pipes were clear. They fished one of her oversized dresses and some pants out of the sewer outlet, near the cottage. The women had to spend all day Sunday cleaning their rooms of the overflow. She was sent to seclusion, where she was safer until they cooled off. Her senseless tricks kept the place in an uproar. Nobody was sorry to see her go, although obviously she was not a responsible human being. She told me she wanted to be an evangelist.

Another, who was finally sent to Cincinnati, was my little blonde friend. She had lost all her statutory days, had been in seclusion innumerable times. She was kept for a time in medical seclusion in the hospital, but finally returned to No. 26. No other cottage would keep her. Her language was often so vile it disgusted even the most hard-boiled prisoners. Once we all agreed not to talk to her, to try to stop it. After a few days of silence, she went weeping to apologize to women she had reviled. She was anxious to learn and soaked up much information for good or bad. If I used a word she did not know she would ask the meaning of it and try to use it. From this it occurred to me to try to replace her habitual four-letter words with some scientific terms. I got the dictionary and explained them to her; words like anus, excrement, urine, intercourse, etc. She had fun trying them out on others. "They think I'm talking a foreign language," she said.

One day I showed her a robin's nest on the front of the cottage. The mother bird was frantically feeding her young, who were so big they were crowding each other out of the nest. My friend shouted at them, "Stay in there, wait till your mommy teaches you to fly!" Inmates passing by stared in wonder. She seemed to be talking to the side of the house. They asked, "What are you doing?" and she answered, "Talking to the birds!" They shook their heads, fearing she was losing her mind. I saw her spend a whole day tinkering with an old clock she found discarded in the waste basket in an officer's room. It was strictly contraband but she made it run. Another day an officer took her for a ride in a truck. She helped move furniture all day and came back happy.

One day Miss Kinzella told her she was a "degenerate." She knew all the vile words for lesbianism but not this word. "Am I a degenerate, Elizabeth?" she asked. "According to the rules of normal decent society you are," I replied, "if you do all the things you are accused of doing." She defended herself by saying her mother was a prostitute and a lesbian and she was brought up that way! In a fit of anger she wrote to Mr. Bennett and asked to be transferred to Cincinnati. The Alderson authorities gladly agreed. While they were making the arrangements they allowed her to come down to my basement sewing room, with me. She would sit in a little rocking chair, knitting and singing to herself. They brought her a new dress with a heliotrope pattern and new shoes. One day the officer suggested she take a shower and wash her hair, as they might let her go to the movies. I felt apprehensive of these sudden favors. Instead, after supper they locked her in her room.

I did not go to the movies. I listened for a wild outburst. Then I heard her voice calling me, "Elizabeth, they are taking me to Cincinnati." I said, "Ask the officer to unlock me to say goodbye," which she did, glad to have me talk to my friend. I urged her to be good for the ten months left so she could go home to her baby. She cried and clung to me and said, "I will never forget you." Then she was gone, before the others returned. The only officer she liked was sent with her, accompanied by a male guard. I heard that she behaved beautifully on the train. The officer said, "Everybody will think you are my daughter." She played the part well, pretending the guard was "Pop." I also heard from another officer that there had been a proposal to give her a place in the basement with me, to let her repair chairs and tables and do odd jobs. I'm sure it could have worked. I missed her and was sorry it had not come to pass.

I had the deepest sympathy for these young so-called incorrigibles. They were usually from institutions, never had a decent childhood or family life, had been kicked and buffeted around. Another such, was a sturdy and strong young Negro girl from the deep South. She trusted no one, made no friends and was quick to defend herself. Her naive, outspoken ways made her the object of ridicule and teasing by Northern smart-alecks, both white and Negro. They were often very cruel. One day I heard her ask an officer, "Miss W are you married?" (For some obscure reason all officers in Alderson were "Miss," even pregnant ones and those whose husbands called for them daily). The officer replied, "Yes, I am." The girl said: "I'd like to get married. But in here they say you must marry a girl." The officer flushed, then said calmly: "Oh they're just kidding you. You'll meet a nice man some day and then you'll get married." This pleased her very much. She said to me later, "Did you ever hear of such a crazy thing?" I said, "Miss W is right. It's all nonsense. Don't listen to them." But over this and other matters she was involved in many fights and was finally taken away.

One we were all glad to see go was the stool pigeon who had made the trouble for me in Cottage 26. The most universally despised women in Alderson were the stool pigeons.

Another young woman who had a bad time had participated in an armed robbery of a bank in the South, in which her husband killed a man. She turned state's evidence against him and he was hanged. She got a stiff sentence but boasted she had saved her neck. She was shunned and despised by the other inmates.

Another stool pigeon who was in Alderson when we arrived was Barbara Hartle from Seattle, Washington. She had been convicted there in a Smith Act case, as a Communist Party local official. While in jail awaiting bail, she became an informer for the FBI. It was the irony of fate and retributive justice, that she waived her appeal and was sent to prison. Under a later decision of the U.S. Supreme Court, the Seattle Smith Act case was dismissed and no other defendant went to prison. When we arrived the other inmates did not know her history, but were suspicious of her because she was taken out often on mysterious trips. She appeared as a government witness against John Hellman of Montana, whose case was later dismissed; against defendants in Denver; in the McCarran Act hearings; in deportation cases, and many other proceedings.

Barbara Hartle drove the truck of the dairy cottage known as the Maples, which was quite a distance out. When Betty first went to work in the storehouse, this woman came to deliver milk and pick up supplies. She said, "Hello, Betty," and tried to talk to her. But Betty, who was uniformly courteous to all, turned her back on her, to the surprise of the others. After she left they asked, "Betty, what's wrong?" She told them how she had caused teachers and workers in plants of the Northwest to lose their jobs, had caused others to be threatened with prison and deportation. They were horrified and exclaimed, "The dirty stool pigeon!" After that she got a cold shoulder from all in the storehouse.

When Betty felt that the hard manual work in the storehouse was too much for her, she had spoken to the elder Miss Smithson, who was then the dietitian in Alderson, and a

severe but just woman. She appreciated Betty's superior intelligence and requested that she be transferred to her department, to help keep the records. Instead Barbara Hartle
was assigned to Miss Smithson. But this shoddy piece of
favoritism on the part of the administration did not help her.

Stool pigeons may be heroes in the press and on TV. But
it is hard to glorify cowards and double-dealers, interested
only in saving themselves and making money. Even those who
use them despise them. In prison they are soon isolated. One
day Barbara Hartle drove a dairy girl over to our cottage to
live. I spoke to this new girl about her. She said, "Now I
know how things we said on the truck, by ourselves, got back
to the officers." Finally Hartle was taken out to testify and
did not return. She teaches now in an anti-Communist school
run by Reverend Billy Hargis, one of the ultra-Right
fanatics.

[25]

Lesbianism in Alderson

Anyone who is reasonably well-read has heard of lesbianism, a term originating from the isle of Lesbos in Greece
where the poetess Sappho wrote sonnets to the love of one
woman for another. But few of us had ever encountered it on
the outside and had little notion of the extent to which it
existed. Like homosexuality among men, it is mostly identified with institutions where one sex is segregated for long
periods of time. One of the girls in the House of Detention
said to Dorothy Day, editor of the *Catholic Worker:* "Here
we are treated like animals. So why shouldn't we act like animals?" Miss Day pointed out to her that this is a libel on the

animals, as perversion does not exist among them. Dorothy Day gave the clearest description of one of the foulest two-word expressions used in prison, referring to one's mother. She wrote: "They go all the way back to Oedipus and accuse each other of knowingly committing the crime which he unwittingly committed and for which he endured the voluntary penance of putting out his eyes." Yet this horrible word was heard day and night in the prison.

A popular saying in Alderson went as follows: "They work us like a horse, feed us like a bird, treat us like a child, dress us like a man—and then expect us to act like a lady." Sometimes as I sat in the auditorium at a movie or music appreciation I thought a bust of Sappho would be far more appropriate than the grim-faced father of his country, who looked down from his pedestal. The women walked two-by-two, as directed by the officer. But they chose their own partners and woe betide anyone who tried to cut in on an unmistakable lesbian pair. The masculine type had close-cropped hair, slicked down tight with oil, and was often called "him." It was hard not to call some of them "him." The slacks were starched to a fare-thee-well, with a crease like a knife and cuffs turned up just so; the shirt was black or blue. This outfit, like a uniform, appeared all along the lines. In the dark of the movies these pairs held hands and kissed passionately, and walking home hung behind the lines, behaving in a lover-like fashion.

There were some "masculine" inmates of Alderson who never wore a dress except at the Sunday noon meals, when it was obligatory. Then it was the darkest possible and it was changed immediately afterwards. It was noticeable that this type were quite often homely, as women; flat chested, narrow hipped, no curves, sometimes extremely thin. They actually looked better in masculine-like attire and probably wore men's sports clothes outside. At a distance they looked like boys. One shortsighted old lady visitor demanded of an officer, "What's that good-looking boy doing here?" Those who had been lesbians in the outer world, were usually less aggressive and flaunting about it than the new recruits. Others, who took it up in prison—as a "pastime," they said— were often married women with husbands and children outside, who resumed their normal family life upon release. One such sent news of her pregnancy to an officer, causing hysterical consternation on the part of her prison "lover," to whom she had promised to be true.

Some of these pairs became extremely involved emotionally. In one instance, one forced the other to tear up her husband's picture and to stop writing to him. Jealousy was rampant and brutal assaults and fights resulted. Such couples were inseparable; in the movies, at church, or walking to work, to the dining rooms, to the library, craft shop, or commissary. They called each other "husband" and "wife," and exchanged rings. I was told of one couple who had issued invitations to a "wedding," shortly before we came here, and were sent to seclusion in punishment. The lesbians made elaborate plans to meet outside and live together, most of which meant nothing. The masculine partner dominated the relationship, demanding and getting service. Their clothes were washed and ironed for them, their rooms cleaned, presents made or bought, and commissary provided. I knew one girl who worked it like a racket, playing one admirer against another, while she laughed and told me privately of her true friend outside, to whom she would return.

This woman told me an interesting story of her life. Her father was a prize-fighter, a widower. He dressed his girls in boy's clothes and taught them to box. She said she felt embarrassed and undressed in girl's clothes. She and her sister, both in Alderson, were lesbians. She sat on the little porch at the back of Cottage 26 with me, in the cool of the evening, and told me of a girl friend of hers outside whom she had loved very much. But her friend fell in love with a young man, who deserted her after she was pregnant. My Alderson friend heard of her plight and took her back. She got a job as an agricultural worker to be able to take care of the friend and put her in a hospital when the baby came. "She walked the floor like a daddy," her sister laughingly interrupted. When the little boy was about five years old, the mother got married, this time for keeps. But the boy would come to see his "other mother" regularly. The sister, who had two children, a very pretty and bright girl, had sold dope. So this one who wanted a nice home for her current girl friend—"TV, record player, sitting room suite"—etc., decided that work was alright, but she needed fast money. So she began to sell the little drug packages, like her sister did. She swore she'd never do it again, and I believe she meant it. She worked on the farm and later in the paint crew, was strong and energetic and not afraid of work. She was the one for whom I wrote the letter, which enabled her to be transferred to the paint crew.

I cannot say if all the prostitutes in Alderson were lesbians. Certainly all lesbians were not prostitutes. The attitude of the prostitute towards sex reflected their twisted and sordid lives outside. It was something to sell and they would do it in prison too, if it were profitable. The benefits they could reap, and not affection, swayed them. They frankly discussed the pimp system outside, where sometimes lesbians are pimps too. If several prostitutes worked for the same male pimp they referred to each other as "wives-in-law." Many of the prostitutes did not like work. They described their lives outside as drinking, smoking, sometimes drugs, playing cards, listening to the radio and TV, preferably jazz, lolling around, waiting for their male customers. Except for the lack of drinking, drugs, and men, they managed to create an atmosphere in a cottage living room which was not too different. The conversations were usually of their life outside, of their friends, and what they planned to do. Some seemed to lack completely any moral sense and revelled in filthy language. Others were clean-spoken, neat in their persons, did good work in the craft shop, and went to church. As they approached their release dates, anxiety and shame at facing their parents or growing children, would often overwhelm the latter group.

Some officers were greatly disturbed by the prevalence of lesbianism, especially as it spread to younger inmates. They talked to them, but their efforts were usually fruitless. They were laughed at as "prudes." Miss Smithson once cancelled a dozen out of an evening class, when they came in couples, in the typical attire, sitting together, and whispering love talk, as they pretended to work. Individual officers could do very little about this all too prevalent problem. Old and young, first-termers, many there for offenses not involving moral turpitude, most of whom had never met or heard of such people in their lives, were thrown in with tough, seasoned criminals and perverts, addicts, prostitutes, dope peddlers, and the like. They were often terrified of the perverts and with good cause. This was especially true in the dormitories, I was told, where conversations and actions were unrestrained, once the doors were locked. These dormitories were seedbeds of degeneracy. What happened to one young girl there, an officer described to me as "actual rape." These dormitories should be made over into individual rooms. And those known to be lesbians should be isolated from the young and first offenders. Prisons are not a cure but schools for every sort of evil.

It was sad to see the change that took place in some of the girls who were in orientation with us, in their appearance, behavior, and language. In a few months, gentle girls took on a rough hard-boiled attitude, cut their long hair, and adopted lesbianism as a fad, a novelty, a diversion, or as defiance. Some would be ashamed when they met us. One said to me: "Please don't tell Betty how I look and act now. She thought I was such a nice girl." But none of them would be specific as to what she did. I tried to probe as to what the practices were but was not successful. At a certain point in the conversation shame overcame them or they lacked words, and they would stop talking. In fact I learned more after I came out from reading *The Second Sex* by Simone de Beauvoir than I did in Alderson.

However, I was given many strange reasons why they indulged in lesbianism. I do not vouch for their veracity but I will list them. Some women claimed that it arose from the sudden cessation of their sexual life and the resultant craving. Such concepts as self-control, discipline, or sublimation were foreign to them, especially those who boasted that they were high-powered sexually. One woman, who worked beside me at the sewing table remarked, "I had all the sex I wanted outside and I'm going to get all I want in here." Sunday mornings I would see her dressed in her choir robes, looking prim and demure.

Some, like the little Negro girl in our shop, had a horror of men. Incestuous fathers and brutal husbands had contributed to a hatred of sex as practiced by men. Fear of pregnancy affected others. One weary woman, who had a large family, a child each year, and now had a long sentence, said, "Well at least I won't have any more kids for a while." Some spoke of the roughness and coarseness of men in the sex act and lack of satisfaction for women. Not only did the inmates accuse each other of lesbianism (and no one was safe from a normal ordinary friendship being distorted by slander) but they accused the officers, as well. Two women officers who were transferred to Terminal Island were characterized as lesbians quite generally by the inmates of Alderson.

I saw an example of such an accusation in Cottage 26. The most masculine type of woman I have ever seen came there for disciplinary reasons. She had a boy's name. She impressed me as one who required an operation to remedy some mistake of nature. It was hard not to automatically say "He" of this person. Outside she had used a man's name, dressed as a man, and was arrested for eloping over a state border with a teenage girl. But her older sister saved her from a most serious charge by identifying her as a woman, a product of a broken home and institutional life since she was a child. She was a hard worker and the officer took her around to hang curtains, wash windows, empty trash, clean up the garret and the cellar. The inmates did not like this officer, who was a bullying slavedriver type. Gossip began about these two until it reached the head office. One day the "girl" was yanked off the line at commissary and sent, without explanation, to seclusion. The officer was given a long leave of absence until the talk blew over and the "girl" had left.

Officers had to be careful to show no favoritism or particular interest in an inmate. This was unfortunate as the more mature ones could have helped some youngsters. But the atmosphere was so polluted with this corrupting influence that it created an atmosphere of fear and intimidation. The attitude of the administration was evasive and equivocal. Not one but several officers told me that Miss Kinzella would not allow any reference to lesbianism, let alone a discussion of it at officers' conferences or meetings with the administration. Whatever the reason, possibly a squeamish puritanism, her policy apparently was to ignore this all pervasive condition. Inmates cynically concluded that it was alright if you didn't get caught in the act, and they would say it was tolerated because it helped keep the women "quiet." I do not know the answers as to remedies. But conjugal visits, such as are allowed in Mexican and Latin American prisons, would certainly help.

Dr. Harris faced this problem by keeping the women busy in healthy and interesting outdoor activities, such as tennis, basket ball, volley ball, dancing, individual gardening, hikes around the reservation. Such activities should be reinstated. She also permitted concerts, style shows, quiz contests, mass singing, prizes for the best cottage, honor cottages, farewell parties—all calculated to keep the women busy and happier. In men's prisons correspondence courses in many subjects are permitted. None were allowed at Alderson, up to the time I left. Nor were there any pre-release programs for long-termers, to help them readjust to the outside world, as there are in some men's prisons. Dr. Harris summed it up in her book: "Entertainment and diversions are actually means of self-preservation in an institution such as ours, and an important outlet for the repressed life inevitable in confinement."

At Alderson, when I was there and from all reports I have received since, I have no reason to believe it is any better now. Detention was the main purpose, punishment the main emphasis. Rehabilitation is missing completely. I doubt if anyone ever came out of Alderson a better person than they were when they entered. Life in prison should be made as normal as possible. Even we who were politicals, with a firm grip on our minds and spirit, were affected in health, and can never forget the petty annoyances, the humiliating treatment, the rank injustices, the frustrations, the avoidable human suffering, and the evil atmosphere of this whited sepulcher of a place.

[26]

Addicts at Alderson

I refused to pass judgment on either lesbians or addicts. I did not believe that either group were criminals. Rather, society should sit in judgment on a system that creates such conditions and people. I pitied almost everyone in prison and tried to understand them. The dope addicts seemed the most helpless and hopeless. I was not in a position to fathom completely the heredity, environment, social pressures, sickness, or injustice which had brought them there. It was obvious that the majority were poor, from the slums of the big cities. A wise man once wrote:

"Poverty is like a foreign country. Only those who have lived there know anything about it; other people don't even seem to give it a thought. And when they do happen to say anything about it they say the sort of thing they would about a country they have never seen, in other words they talk nonsense. People who have always had enough to eat and always had a bed to sleep in, should not be allowed to discourse on what they would or would not have done, had they been poor. They are like men who talk about war without having been in the trenches." (Albert Londres, *Road to Buenos Ayres,* Liveright, 1928.)

Of course it would not be correct to say that all addicts are poor. But the rich ones seldom land in prison. At Alderson there were several nurses, one the wife of a doctor who was taking the cure at the hospital in Lexington; there were several women who had been in the armed services; there were some who started the habit in school. The most famous addict prisoner, who had been there before we came, was Billie Holiday, a Negro woman, who was one of the greatest blues singers. She served a year and a day in Alderson on a narcotics charge. While there she endeared herself to the inmates by refusing to sing for a party of guests at the Warden's residence, saying under her contract she was not allowed to sing free. But she could sing for charity, so she offered to sing for the inmates, which was refused. Her *New York Times* obituary notice on July 18, 1959, when she died at 44, described her as one who "became a singer from desperation rather than desire. . . . She was the daughter of a 13-year old mother and a 15-year old father. . . . The first major influence on her singing came when as a child she ran errands for the girls in a nearby brothel in return for the privilege of listening to recordings of Louis Armstrong and Bessie Smith. . . . She came into stardom in 1938, when she appeared at Café Society. There she introduced one of her best known songs:

'Strange Fruit', a biting description of a lynching, written by Lewis Allen."

After her release from Alderson she was unable to get a cabaret license, because of her conviction. Narcotic agents hounded her last years. Even when she was dying in a hospital, with lung congestion and heart failure, she was placed under arrest on a charge of possession of narcotics and a police guard stood over her, until a judge ordered him removed. This beautiful and talented woman said: "I've been told nobody sings the word 'hunger' like I do, or the word 'love.' All I've learned is wrapped up in those two words." She wrote her own epitaph when she said, "There isn't a soul on this earth who can say for sure that their fight with dope is over until they are dead."

To my knowledge I had never met an addict in the outside world. It was a shock, at first, to have a quiet, intelligent, well-mannered, young Negro woman tell me, "I am an addict," and that she began to use narcotics at Wadleigh High School in New York City. She was not the only one who started as a student, at the instigation of older girls who bought the stuff at a nearby candy store. I met another who told me the story of herself and her brother, both college graduates. One parent was white, the other colored. When they asked her color on the entrance questionnaire at Alderson, she answered, "Suit yourself." They put her down as colored. She said with a bitter laugh: "Elizabeth, that's our story. Everywhere we go we are colored. My brother, an engineering student, could only get a job running an elevator. I could only get domestic work, standing on the street in the Bronx where they called it 'the slave market.' Our education was worthless to us." Finally they sought refuge in the dream world of drugs. I tried to talk to her about the Negro liberation movement and how young people should enlist in it. But it was too late. She was in the grip of an escape from reality through narcotics and had no fight left. Rather she was marking time to get out and have the first "fix."

Poor people who become addicts become so enmeshed in the underworld machinery they are not able to extricate themselves. Drugs are very costly and daily the amount must be found. To be able to satisfy the horrible craving for the drug, without which they suffer the tortures of the damned, they often become peddlers or pushers. It is an apt term, because they deliberately lure others into using it, especially the young and foolish looking for thrills. Once "hooked" the new converts become a source of steady funds to the pusher. Lack of money leads to desperation and crime; stealing from families and friends, and finally anywhere they can find either the drug or money. Doctors and druggists are held up, sometimes killed, to get drugs. Narcotics are stolen in hospitals and even in jails and prisons. This had happened in Alderson where nurses' aides who were addicts were caught stealing patients' medicine, substituting water or sugar pills. There were a number of addicts in prison for stealing drugs in hospitals where they had been employed as nurses or orderlies.

An order came through from Washington that no addicts were allowed to work in the prison hospital, in any capacity. The small-time pushers and addicts in Alderson chummed together and talked their own junkie language, which was incomprehensible to a "square." There was fear of their outside underworld higher-up, which curtailed their confidences to non-addicts.

Occasionally one heard tales that revealed this constant fear. One woman told me of a friend of hers who had "squealed" to the narcotics agents on whoever had sold her the drug in quantity. They gave her a "hot" needle she said, presumably poison, which caused her death. Another was in a frantic state of mind while she was with us in orientation. We thought it was from being in prison. But she told me that it was something else. A friend of hers was an addict. Her husband was trying to cure her and had ordered all her friends not to give her any dope. But this woman felt sorry for her and gave her a supply. Apparently it had not been properly cut or diluted and it killed her. She was grief-stricken over her friend and frightened of what the husband would do, if he learned the facts. Death lurks very near for addicts, pushers, and peddlers. The higher-ups, who are usually not addicts but gangsters, will brook no nonsense. It is a million-dollar racket for them. Their long shadows reach into prisons, to either help people get out or keep them there. Fear as well as habit leads many back on the same path after their release. They are truly "hooked."

No matter how injurious the effects of the drug, the addicts were convinced it was beneficial. This was one reason that mere deprivation of the drugs does not "cure," any more than alcoholics are cured by being denied liquor. The craving remained. The first "fix," the first drink, were engrossing topics of prison conversation. They boasted that they were never sick a day, on the street, while using the stuff while "Here I am sick all the time." They talked wistfully of how much calmer, brighter, happier they were when on drugs. One woman told me how much quicker she could do a crossword puzzle while under their influence. It was horrifying to hear them tell wide-eyed youngsters "how good a fix will be for you." But they are obsessed, rather than vicious. Long prison terms are certainly not remedies for women who are obviously emotionally disturbed and unbalanced, who are not criminals but sick.

In the House of Detention in New York, when addicts were first arrested, they were given what is called the "cold turkey" treatment—thrown into the tank floor and taken completely off the drug. They became violently ill, vomited, had chills, and nearly died. Some did. Prior to a long prison term they may be sent to the hospital at Lexington to be "cured." There are 60,000 addicts in the United States, according to the Bureau of Narcotics. Lexington has a capacity for 1,280. By the time they arrived at Alderson, the worst stages of withdrawal were over. But there is no basic cure other than abstinence. The addicts know it. Threat of punishment does not deter them. Possession is punishable by five to ten years imprisonment for a first offense. Suspended sentences and parole are denied. Life or death sentences are possible in extreme cases. Yet the compulsion for the drug is such that even this does not stop the majority of them.

Since I came out of Alderson I have read considerably on the subject of drug addiction, and am convinced my conclusions there were correct. Such books as *Who Live in Shadows* (McGraw-Hill, 1959), by Chief Magistrate John M. Murtagh and Mrs. Sarah Harris, a social worker, advocate the abolition of stiff sentences for addicts and a federally operated system of outpatient clinics, at which addicts would receive necessary narcotics under medical supervision. To Commissioner Henry L. Anslinger, who headed the Narcotics Division for over 30 years and has recently retired—unwillingly—at 70, addiction is a police control problem, to be repressed with the greatest severity. Alexander King, the writer, characterized him as follows: "His name will eventually go down in medical history as one of the major stumbling blocks to an enlightened policy in the field of human rehabilitation." (*May This House Be Safe from Tigers*, Simon and Shuster, 1960). Anslinger admitted that $350,000,000 is spent annually on drugs. Evidently his sadistic concepts of cruel punishment were not successful, but he ranted and raved at all proposed changes.

I heard some discussions as to remedies, by addicts. They told me that in England there are about 400 addicts. There is no compulsory treatment and doctors are permitted to dispense drugs at proscribed nominal prices. "Gee, if I could only get to England," was a common remark. They told me that there were police quotas for arrests in New York City. Later, in 1959, this accusation was confirmed by the head of the narcotics squad, who retired at 50 because he said they were pressured to make a certain number of arrests, regardless of the circumstances. Addicts also told me that addict stool pigeons or informers who give information to the au-

thorities, were supplied with drugs by the police and narcotics agents. This too was confirmed in a recently published
report, *Drug Addiction: Crime or Disease?* by a joint committee of the American Bar Association and the American
Medical Association (Indiana University Press). Their conclusions are in accord with other qualified experts, that a new
medical approach should be considered, that long prison
terms for addicts be abolished, that dispensation by doctors
be allowed, and that an experimental clinic be established.
The report cites the success of such practices in England and
other European countries. Addicts would not then be either
the pariahs or the victims they are today, the prey of informers and gangsters. I was glad to see that our trial judge,
Edward S. Dimock, was a member of this humane committee.

Serving brutally long terms and left to their own devices,
some weird and dangerous habits developed among addicts
in Alderson, in their reckless search for narcotics and "kicks."
One day a notice appeared on the bulletin board, signed by
Miss Kinzella, warning that the fluid used to clean the typewriters was a deadly poison and if it were sniffed by anyone
could cause serious damage to the nose, throat, and respi-
ratory system. If taken internally, it could cause death. Several
women were already sick in the hospital from sniffing it. Another woman had smoked the teeth of a plastic comb. She
nearly died, her heart and lungs were permanently injured,
and she became so thin her husband did not recognize her
when he came to see her. When partially recovered she was
allowed to come to the craft shop to work but lived in Davis
Hall, under constant surveillance. She was given special food
to try to build her up and was not allowed to smoke cigarettes, which caused her to choke and even to pass out. She
begged the other women for cigarettes but after seeing the
results a few times, they were frightened and refused. She was
allowed only a metal comb and all plastic articles were kept
away from her. She was a pitiful sight when she was released,
especially as she had come in a robust woman.

Rumors and Humors

Nothing spreads in a prison as fast as a rumor, and by some odd system of "grape vine," possibly letters from husbands in other prisons, rumors even came from far away institutions. Some came from newspaper stories, as when one day an inmate rushed up to me, all excited. "You're going to get out, Elizabeth," she said. "Well," I said in surprise, "how come? I haven't heard of it." "Oh, yes," she said confidently, "Mrs. Roosevelt said so." Some one had showed her a newspaper item that Mrs. Roosevelt, along with a large group of liberals, had urged amnesty for me and all other Smith Act prisoners. I said, "That's wonderful," and did not disillusion her. I only wished Mrs. F.D.R. had the power. There were constant rumors of Mr. Bennett's resignation. He had been appointed in a Democratic administration and the inmates were sure he would be dumped by the Republicans. "It's a nice fat, juicy job," they would say. But Mr. Bennett is still there.

One day in April of 1955 a girl came running into the dining room, screaming "Billy Ekstine died." I did not know who he was but they exclaimed—"tops, as a blues singer." There was much grief. The next day I got my New York paper and saw that Albert Einstein had died. They did not know Einstein any more than I had known Ekstine. So when I explained, there was great relief, even rejoicing. The loss of the great scientist meant nothing to them.

There was always special interest in the lifers, and there were at least six there then. Rumors would fly about their possible release. Three were wives of American soldiers. Two had murdered their husbands in overseas bases. Another was accused of killing three of her children, while temporarily insane at a lonely army base in Eritrea, Africa. All of these women had been tried by army courts-martial, although they were civilians and the last was a British subject. Later the U.S. Supreme Court reversed itself and decided that such military trials were unconstitutional in capital cases, and the women should have been returned to the United States for trial in civil courts. One of the women involved was the daughter of a U.S. general. The women did not begrudge them their release when it came, especially the young mother whose husband had stood by her gallantly and was waiting for her outside, with their one surviving daughter. But the women made wisecracks like: "I should have killed my old man instead of selling the stuff. I'd get out quicker!"

Another interesting case of a soldier's wife, who did not get out, was a woman who had married a dozen soldiers to collect their allotments. This vastly intrigued the women. "Why didn't I think of that?" they would joke. Very few inmates had a real sense of humor. What passed for humor was crude, usually vulgarity and smut about sex. Occasionally, however, a piece appeared in *The Eagle* that was an excellent example of lively humor. But I never had the good fortune to meet the writers. Usually it was a bit risky to joke, as they either took it absolutely seriously or were insulted. They had a joke on me about my contraband tomatoes, big ripe ones, that one of the women brought me regularly from the kitchen. I was afraid to leave them in the cottage and could not eat them all at once. So I would lug them in my little utility bag to the shop and back and try to get someone to share them.

They were hilarious over some moonshine made at Christmas time and discovered behind Miss Kinzella's house, especially as the culprits were not found. Our cottage moonshiners were not so lucky. One day, near my last Christmas, I came back from work to discover all four women on the floor with me had been sent to seclusion. When I inquired from the officer what had happened she said, "It has nothing to do with you." They had been making moonshine for Christmas. They took fruit and sugar from the kitchen and a large jar from the hospital, and started it quite a while before. They had hidden the jar in the cellar, behind a broken partition. But a cat squeezed in and could not get out. It cried day and night until guards were sent to rescue it and they found the crock with the fermenting contents. The officer said to the women lined up for supper, "It was awful stuff. You're lucky you did not get it," and they asked her: "How do you know? Did you taste it?" The girls were released for Christmas but bemoaned their loss and cursed that cat. "You'd have had the first drink, Elizabeth," they said. Maybe the cat did me a favor.

One of the most tiresome things in prison was the catch-phrases they would pick up and work to death, like "See you later, alligator" or "Later for you!" I got so weary of all the pet names they called each other—baby, doll, honey, darling, sugar. On one thing I was adamant, I allowed no one to call me "mom." I explained I had lost my only son and I could not bear to hear the word, which sufficed to stop it. Another tiresome business was the repetitive songs on the radio. They knew how to find every program of popular songs. One, however, which became a regular theme song of Alderson was very mournful with a fine melody, written by Alex North. It was called, "Unchained Melody." But I never want to hear most of them again. I could take the jazz and blues, but not the hill-billy songs or preachers.

Another rumor that spread throughout the prison was that the priest, as a member of the official administration, told what he heard in the confessional. The attendance at church, and especially the confessions fell off. One of the Catholic Puerto Rican politicals discussed it with the priest, since confession was a good outlet for the women and the priest gave them sensible advice. Shortly afterwards he published in his weekly bulletin an article entitled, "Father Never Tells," which reassured everyone.

I got a book about trees from the library. As a city-bred person I hardly knew one tree from another. In the Summer of 1956, when I had more freedom, I would take the book with me whenever I went out and would try to identify the trees. I must have looked odd with my open book to the women who passed. They would say: "What are you doing, Elizabeth? Reading to the trees?" I tried another book on the birds and am sure by that time some of them thought my mind was affected. "She's reading to a robin,—loco!" one friend said sadly.

By then I was losing weight quite rapidly and the girls in the hospital, where I went to be weighed, said "Elizabeth, you're getting to be a slick chick! You ought to be able to catch a beau now!"

Romance was always a subject of great interest. But I was amazed that they did not like the movie "Marty," which was so popular outside. They wanted glamor, not ordinary plain-looking people, as in that story. I went occasionally in my second year to see Frank Sinatra, Danny Kaye, "The Little Kidnappers" and a few others rated as good in my papers. But occasionally parts were censored out, which was very annoying. I felt smothered with women at the movie and usually preferred to stay in the cottage. I wrote a poem called "How I'd like to see a Man," which amused my friends there. They were very curious about my correspondent, Dr. Clemens France, whose picture I had on my bureau. "Boy, he's good looking! Are you going to marry him?" they would ask. When I laughed and said "No," they would try to persuade me. "You ought to settle down at your age. You'll only get into more trouble if you keep on with your work! Let somebody else do it!" they would urge.

They were greatly interested in any reference to me in a paper or magazine. The *New Republic* had an editorial criticizing my imprisonment under the Smith Act, but said I was just "a mouse" compared to the government. They got a big kick out of that. One day in the Spring of 1957, when the Communist Party was holding a convention, an officer called me into the side storeroom of the shop. She said, "Elizabeth I saw something in the paper about you being elected to a Board of Directors." Having myself seen it in *The Times,* I asked, "Was it the Communist Party?" But she could not recall, so little did "Communist" mean to these backwoods housewives. She seemed to think it must be a great honor because it was in the paper.

[28]

Racial Discrimination

Even after the cottages were desegregated by law, discrimination and prejudice did not come to an end. The Negro women were assigned, as before, to all the menial tasks; on the farm, in the cannery, in the laundry, on maintenance, and at the piggery until it was abolished. The cannery was seasonable and it meant hard work until the fresh fruit and vegetables were put up. Many Negro women from the North were capable of skilled and clerical work, but were not so assigned.

When we first went down to see our lawyers, Mrs. Kaufman and Mr. Abt, in the main building, the absence of any Negro women on the large stenographic and typing staff of the front office was conspicuous. Finally, a Negro woman, who came to serve a short sentence for alleged tax evasion, was assigned there. She was one of Congressman Adam Powell's secretaries from New York and her case had all the earmarks of a political frame-up. Strangely enough, her period of orientation was very short, she was assigned to one of the best cottages on the lower campus, sang in the choir, and worked as a typist in the front office. The Negro women attributed this to the publicity the Congressman could give the place. Also, they noted she was extremely light and not too easily identified as a Negro. Some did not like her when she was heard to say she did not need straightener for her hair. They were extremely sensitive to such remarks.

She was paroled at the earliest possible date and I am sure she left with illusions as to the place, since she was treated exceptionally well. I had sent her copies of my New York papers and some of the Negro inmates suggested I talk to her before she left about conditions there. I met her one day on the way back from commissary, introduced myself and told her that I hoped she realized that her treatment was not typical of the Negro women. I suggested she investigate before she left so she could tell the Congressman some of the bad things that happened to Negro women there. But she was extremely nervous even talking to me and excused herself almost immediately. I never saw anywhere that she spoke up for the women of her race after she left. Less fortunate Negro women who had neither friends nor access to publicity, watched for it too and were much disappointed.

The degree of illiteracy was higher among Negro women from the South. They were rarely addicts but usually family women whose "crimes" were not of moral turpitude but of a lesser degree. They were women from farms or workers from cities, hard-working women, more solid in character and sober of mind than many of their Northern city sisters. In the last few years, when so many more government checks were floating around—social security, for veterans and the like— the percentage of theft that came under federal law had greatly increased. Quite a few were in for that. Others were in for moonshine, a federal offense.

The majority at that time knew little or nothing of the struggle for equal rights for Negro Americans. Probably now, with the Freedom Riders, they would know more. I talked to the Negro women in my cottage about the struggle being waged at that time by Miss Autherine Lucy, a young Negro student who sought admission to Alabama University. Some were pleased, but others said suspiciously, "Why does she try to go where she is not wanted?" and were surprised at my vehemence when I replied, "Because she has a right to go there like anybody else!" They would then say more courageously, "maybe you're right."

I was known as Claudia's friend, even after she left, so I could talk more freely with the Negro women than most white women. They trusted me too as a Communist. I did not blame them for being careful. They had been double-crossed so often. They were exploited by the administration and inmates alike. White women from the South were particularly obnoxious, expecting Negro women to wait on them and work for them, treating them rudely and contemptuously. I heard of one white woman who proposed to a Negro woman "friend" that she be the pimp to find customers and the Negro woman be the prostitute. This was the first time I heard of a lesbian acting as a pimp, but there were quite a few, I was told, and I read of it later.

Claudia Jones was greatly respected by all the Negro inmates. They were proud of her achievements, her talent, and her bold independent spirit, as they had been proud of Billie Holiday. We were both outraged at what appeared to be a crude and vulgarly offensive form of white-supremacist attitudes, or what we called "white chauvinism" masquerading as "love," in interracial lesbian relations. The whites took full advantage of the Negro women involved. Claudia was in a position to speak out indignantly, and she did to the Negro women. She pointed out to them how some Southern white women behaved with the Negro women there as they did with Negro men, in the South. They often evinced a fascination or attraction for Negro men, chased after them, intimidated them, and compromised them. But if the relationship was discovered the women cried "rape" and the Negro man was the victim of lynching, castration, or arrest and execution. This was what happened to Willie McGee, in Mississippi. His wife came North and told the tragic story, but to no avail. The white woman, whom everybody in the town knew had been intimate with him, sent him to his death by her accusations.

Claudia had a discussion one day with two bright, attractive young Negro women, who were prison lesbians. She spoke severely to them of how disgraceful their conduct was and asked "What will you do when you go home?" They both laughed and said: "Go back to our husbands of course. You don't think we care anything about this white trash here, do you? They don't mean a thing to us! We just take them for a ride for what we can get out of it." There was one white woman with two children in an institution, who had lost a large number of days, had been in seclusion several times and finally was placed permanently in Cottage 26, because of her persistent pursuit of Negro women. She chased after everyone of them who came into the cottage. Apparently it was a mania with her. The Negro women invariably despised these white women. They had no illusions as to such "love." There were some fine interracial friendships of a normal and clean character, which were based on respect and equality; and were appreciated as a credit to both races, by all of us.

One day a middle-aged white woman came to Cottage 2. She had a short sentence for check-passing but was in a sad state of nerves. When she saw so many Negro women there and was placed in a double dormitory with a young colored woman, she wept hysterically and protested. The officer tried to calm her and said, "As soon as we have a single room vacant, you can have it!" I realized she had made a very bad impression in the cottage and went to talk to her. I asked her where she came from. Her home was a steel town I had often visited. I asked, "What does your husband do?" She replied, "He's a steel-worker." I asked, "Is he a union man?" She answered, "Of course, all the men are." I asked then, "Aren't there a large number of Negro workers in the plant? Doesn't your husband work with them? Aren't they his brothers in the union? Didn't they help organize the union?" She answered, "Yes, of course, they are good union men!" I said: "So why can't you live and work with Negroes here like your husband does at home? They are nice women here. They will help you in any way they can."

She subsided and we heard no more protests.

When a room was vacated, the officer asked her if she wanted to move. By this time she had become fast friends with her young roommate. "Oh, no!" she said, "I wouldn't leave this child. She's like one of my daughters to me, I wouldn't hurt her feelings by moving out." The next day in the shop she laughed and said: "Wasn't I a silly goose when I first came. I've sure learned a lot here!" Thus were good relations established.

There was greater solidarity among Negro women, undoubtedly a result of life outside, especially in the South. It seemed to me they were of better character, by and large, stronger and more dependable, with less inclination to tattle or be a stool pigeon, than the white inmates. Frankly, I trusted the Negro women more than I did the whites. They were more controlled, less hysterical, less spoiled, more mature. I do not mean they did not have any faults. But I felt that the Puerto Rican and Negro women on the whole were less corrupted and more obviously social victims than many of the others. Given a proper environment and opportunity they had all the potentials of honest useful working people. In fact, people in prison are not so different from those outside. There is no prison type. I often see people on the street, on trains, in hotels, that look like and act like women I knew in prison.

A common denominator of the Negro women, which they shared with their people outside, was a sense of good humor with as much laughter as the situation permitted. They were not weepers or complainers, they did not take out their troubles on other people, they were cheerful—not happy, of course, but making the best of things. Singing, dancing beautifully and gracefully in the living room, when the officer permitted it, playing cards. They accepted a bad situation with fortitude. It wasn't easy. Many had children at home or aged parents. Many wept at night. I could hear some who kept up the best front in the daytime, sobbing alone in their room at night. I wrote letters for many of them and came to know some of the sorrow they concealed. But the tragedies of Negro Americans were felt keenly even in a prison; segregation, discrimination, racist ideas of white supremacy, a lack of equality. Like a cancer it gnawed at their lives everywhere. When I returned home I missed the many Negro women, who were my friends in Alderson.

[29]

My Last Year in Alderson

Life had settled into an accustomed routine during 1956, but I marked off the time on the calendar with growing relief and impatience. Kathie came regularly, in cold Winter and hot Summer, bringing me news of my world outside. It was not easy for her, I knew. It was cool there in the mountains even in June and July, especially at night. I wrote very little. What was the use? I could not take it out. I rescued some poems by printing them in *The Eagle,* which I could take home. Others I wrote out in letters. Some I memorized. I had exchanged my pen for needle, thread, pins, and scissors. I was made happy by the news that two good friends were freed of Smith Act charges—Marian Bachrach in New York and Steve Nelson in Pennsylvania. I read a great deal. I found a large book in the library called *Prison Letters.* It was a collection of letters primarily by political prisoners of all countries. I read how Prime Minister Nehru said that he recommended everyone to spend some time in prison, to get a chance to think. He said he wrote some of his best books while there. He at least was considered a political prisoner by the British colonialists. I had no such good fortune.

Betty was in the hospital that Summer and I asked the doctor if I might see her. He said of course. But the authorities said "No." When I saw the doctor next time, as he was leaving the hospital, he asked why I had not come. I said they had refused because we "would talk politics." He was quite disgusted and said, "What's the matter with politics? It's better than what most of them talk around here!" I wondered if I would be able to write again after all the "verbicide" I heard, as Oliver Wendell Holmes called "massacring the language." One day I was particularly annoyed at something and was grumbling to myself as I walked along. A girl asked me, "What's wrong, Elizabeth?" and I replied, "I thought I was coming to a prison, not a darned kindergarten!" She laughed and sprung a standard prison joke: "Well you're alright as long as you just talk to yourself. It's when you start answering yourself that you have to look out!"

I saw reviews of my book in *The New York Times* and *The Nation,* and began to feel closer to the outside. My responsibility in the craft shop had become greater. I kept track of all thread, giving it out to the weavers and tried to be strictly fair to all. But the problem of distribution of the finished products became an increasing vexation. There were six cottages, Davis Hall, the hospital, the library, and classrooms to be serviced on the upper campus. There were twice as many cottages on the lower campus, plus the administration and staff living quarters. Everybody wanted new curtains, place mats, rugs, and the like. Sometimes enterprising officers, when on relief duty in the craft shop, would help themselves to rugs for their cottage. It was chaotic and Miss Smithson tried her best to stop it.

To organize the distribution the administration devised a system that only a prison staff could conjure up. We laughed at it, as we tried to carry it out. An administrative officer not connected with a particular cottage was placed in charge of each campus. She was to order the articles we made, select the colors, and decide the destination. We had to divide all the cones of thread into two parts, making certain that each had identical amounts of the colors and then mark "Miss A" and "Miss H" on each batch. The job fell to me. I felt like King Solomon! Now I had to become a bookkeeper as well, keeping track of which weavers were working on whose orders and what colors they were using. The women were too busy working and too impatient to be bothered. I counted cones of thread, curtains, rugs, table clothes, place mats, and reported to Miss Smithson any shortage of thread. I helped the weavers measure the curtains to finish at the right lengths, and then marked the articles for the receiving officer. We arranged the wares in the closet very neatly so we could open them up to show visitors what was made in the weave shop. Also on display we had a few attractive hooked rugs. The women trusted me not to play favorites and keep them supplied with what they needed. Miss Smithson said she was relieved to be able to deal with an adult and for me it was mutual.

Claudia had helped her in a report on the therapeutic value of the work in the shop, which brought more materials to the shop. I also helped her prepare an estimate of increased needs. We felt that in getting more materials for the shop we were helping the inmates, since everything made there was mainly used in the cottages. I felt better moving around than sitting sewing all day. It was light, clean work and as interesting as anything could be in a prison. But what galled me and shocked everybody else, including officers, was that I never got a single day of good time. I had no hope of it, but both Miss Smithson and my cottage officer urged me to apply and they both recommended it in their monthly reports on each inmate's work, behavior, attitude to others, etc. On my work record and cottage record I was entitled to meritorious days. The officers were indignant and continued to make the recommendation. Each penal institution is supposed to have latitude in deciding on these issues. I had heard from Kathie that some of my male comrades in other prisons were granted meritorious and industrial time and even received pay in connection with special work. But on the whole the uniform rejection in Smith Act cases indicated a national policy. The reason advanced in Alderson was that we did not have the right "attitude," which meant to admit guilt, to show evidence of repentance and rehabilitation. Of course, such an attitude was unthinkable for any one of us. The positions of the prison authorities and ours were diametrically opposed. So we were denied the days we had earned.

This situation verified the remarks which Judge Dimock had made at the time we were called up for sentence, in our trial. I was the first. Judge Dimock said, in effect that he did not expect prison would make any changes in our views. He had allowed all 13 of us to make statements and his conclusion was certainly logical. (Later, speaking at a lawyer's gathering in upstate New York he referred to our remarks in a favorable manner, compared us to the early Christians, and said our speeches should be made a part of judicial history.) To the indignation of the government lawyers, instead of proceeding to sentence, he made us a strange proposition: would we be ready to go to the Soviet Union if it could be arranged? I moved first to reply. I could not confer with my co-defendants, nor could I speak for them, but I said emphatically, "No," and others followed suit. After about three or four had said "No," he said, "Let's forget about it," and proceeded with the sentences.

Later, after the press headlined our refusal as "Reds Prefer Jail to Russia," I asked the judge for permission to make an explanatory statement. Again, over government protest, he consented. I said we would all be happy to visit the Soviet Union. But we would not accept exile from our own country. We did not feel we had any right to go there to enjoy socialism which somebody else had worked to build. "This is our country and our duty is to stay right here and help to build socialism here," I said. Of course, this statement got no headlines. In 1960, when I did visit the Soviet Union, I sent Judge Dimock a New Year's card, that he might know that I finally got there on my own steam, with the right to return freely.

I was happy when the time came in 1956 for Betty to leave, although I knew I would miss her, even if we rarely saw each other. She suggested, through one of my shop mates, that I come to church the last Sunday before she left and she would do likewise. For Betty and I to both go to church caused interest. They kidded us, "Betty and Elizabeth got religion." I asked the officer in our cottage to please put me down for Protestant services. She looked at me keenly, then laughed, "I suppose you are going to meet somebody, Elizabeth, like they all do." She knew Betty and was not really surprised. The girls from Betty's cottage sat near the door and saved a seat for me next to her, which I slipped into. While the minister droned along and the choir sang, we were able to whisper to each other. The women who knew Betty were very fond of her. She was kind and helpful to all. Tears were shed when she left her cottage. When I kissed her goodbye outside, a friendly officer looked the other way, as it was strictly forbidden. I did not feel as bereft as when Claudia left because my own departure seemed much nearer.

By Fall I began to feel I was on my way down the hill too. The holidays came and went, as before. The seasons changed. Spring came, with the great feeling of relief that this was the last one here. I was called to the parole office to sign preliminary release papers. I turned in all my books to the library and began to give away my sweaters, scarfs, handkerchiefs, socks, manicure set, and writing paper. No one had even asked me for it, except an occasional sheet to keep score in card games. I packed small gifts and souvenirs to take home. All letters, except a few, had to be destroyed. I gave away my plants. I mended all my prison clothes, to be turned in the last day. This going out process was prolonged. I felt it was selfish to take out anything which somebody else needed or could use, unless it was a special gift. But not all departing women felt that way. It is quite amazing how some go out with all they can possibly collect, beg, borrow or steal, regardless of the needs of those they called their best friends. A horrible acquisitiveness seemed to possess them, which probably contributed to landing them there in the first place.

I was called to the hospital for a medical check and to Davis Hall, to have another picture taken, for the FBI, I suppose. They claimed I had changed so much in losing 75 pounds, that I looked entirely different from their first picture— which was good news. I was called to the garment shop to be measured and later fitted with going-out clothes, two dresses and a short coat, as it was still quite cool. They were not bad looking, fitted well and could not be identified as prison made. Kathie brought a suitcase with a hat, shoes, stockings, underwear, and left it at the office, to be ready for my dressing out.

Kathie told me an amusing story on one of her visits. Tensions were great among Communists outside after the 16th Convention of the Party in the spring of 1957, due to the exposure of Stalin's cruel methods in the Soviet Union by Nikita Khrushchev at the 20th Congress, and due to other differences. A friend of long standing asked Kathie, "What side is Elizabeth on?" She replied innocently, "Why, don't you know?" He retorted impatiently, "Of course not—that's why I'm asking you." My little sister responded blandly, "She's on the *in*side!" This was all too true. I had little information and could only wait impatiently until I was free, to learn all the details. I was anxious to get into the thick of things again, to help preserve and defend my views and my Party.

I was increasingly impatient, going out fever, it was called. The first group from the Dennis case was released that Spring. I saw their pictures in the paper. One was of Eugene Dennis with John Abt. I put it on my bureau and placed one of Judge Dimock there at the same time. An officer asked, "Who are they?" and I replied, "My judge and my lawyers," so she left them there. It was a joy to see dear Gene's smiling face. With the release of the few men and myself of our case, who had three-year terms, all Smith Act defendants would then be free. Our group unfortunately had the fines, which kept us 30 days longer but that did not mitigate the fine. Mine was $6000 and I am still paying Uncle Sam $10 a month. I figure it will take me another forty-odd years to pay it off. I would then be 113 years old.

I felt sorrowful to leave the women, especially the Puerto Rican politicals, and my first two friends, who were still in Cottage 26. The little cripple girl had become so emotionally disturbed over the detainers, as her release time approached, that she had almost lost her mind and was locked up all the time; "for her own good", they said. The Negro woman A, who still worked in the laundry, would call sorrowfully clear across the campus: "Don't forget to say goodbye, Elizabeth." I had made some real friends there. Even some officers stopped at my cottage to say farewell.

At the very last I had another hassle with Miss Kinzella. I was due to leave on May 25, 1957, a Saturday. When my parole officer noticed the day she was quite disturbed. She said, "I'm afraid you'll have to wait until Monday, Elizabeth," and said in explanation, "Miss Kinzella will not come in to sign papers on Saturdays and Sundays." I was outraged and ready to fight like a tiger for my two days. Nothing had infuriated me so much in all my days there as the idea that this woman presumed to add two days to my sentence. She only lived up the hill from the office, less than five minutes by car. I wrote to Mr. Abt, Clemens France, and Mrs. Kaufman. They called Washington and in a few days I was notified

I would leave on my official last day, May 25, as I had planned. Miss Kinzella was cold as usual, when she signed my papers. But I felt she can't pull that one so easily on any other inmate, after my victory.

The day had come at last. She had set 12 noon as the time, although many left early in the morning. I knew that John Abt, his sister and my friend, Marian Bachrach, and dear sister Kathie would be at the gate, with John's car. On my way down to the garment shop, I met Rosa and was happy to see her. I received all my possessions, including handkerchiefs and books which people had sent without return addresses; my money, and my own book. But my mail was refused to me, as I have already explained.

One of the officers took me to the gate in her car. When I got out I could hear the girls in a cottage on top of the hill, where Carmen lived, shouting, "Goodbye, Elizabeth." I waved to them. The officer and male guard at the gate bade me goodbye. I walked a few yards to my friends and was free at last.

It was a lovely day as we drove through the beautiful West Virginia hills. We came to a nice restaurant. It was a strange feeling to enter it and encounter no curious glances. Apparently, I looked like everybody else again. My only deviation from my normal self was to ask Kathie to buy some gum, probably the most contraband thing at Alderson.

I had permission to stay over night in Washington. Actually, I was not yet legally free. I had to report to a parole officer at Foley Square on Monday morning and was under conditional release until July 6. My Washington friend had a lovely home and had prepared a fine dinner, with whiskey and champagne to celebrate my home coming. But the happiest moment for me was to pick up the *Daily Worker* from her table. I had not seen it since January 1955. I was afraid to drink anything stronger than a little champagne.

Monday I dressed in my blue prison-made dress (nothing else fitted me), and went to see the woman parole officer. I hated to go back to Foley Square, but did stop in to the marshal's office to say hello. Some of them we knew from our eight months' trial. The parole officer was very curious about my impressions of Alderson. She said there were so many conflicting reports. I was cautious, tried to be fair, but felt too close to it not to be critical. She spoke of how short-handed they were in her department, that they could not possibly keep track of all the women when they returned. She warned me, as my parole officer had done in Alderson, not to see any former inmates. "Of course," she said, "you are likely to see your friends!" They both had made a distinction between ex-convicts and my friends who had been in prison, a tacit recognition of our political prisoner status. Later she came to see me at home, rather out of curiosity, I suspected, than from duty. But she was afraid to give me permission to go with Mr. and Mrs. Abt to their Summer place in Kent, Conn., and had to take it up with Washington. I was allowed to go over the July 4th week-end and my conditional release time expired while I was there. Gene Dennis had also received permission to go there. He was still under bail on an untried Smith Act membership indictment, since 1948. We had a real celebration, at last, at my freedom from custody.

Backward Glance on Leaving

It takes a long time to get prison out of one's mind and heart, if at all. As I write I look out at the blue of the San Francisco Bay and the nearby hills. But before me, defacing the lovely bay is one of the most dreaded federal prisons— Alcatraz, called "The Rock," from which three prisoners have just escaped. Possibly only one who has been in prison can fully appreciate the agony the place represents. But good or bad, maximum or minimum, prison is prison. It leaves its mark. For days I awoke at 6 AM and was sleepy at 9 PM. I remembered "Lights out" and at a party, a pleasant dinner or a public meeting, I sadly recalled the women at that hour, locked in their lonely cells and again I shared their sorrow. I am not writing this book to evoke any special sympathy for me or my comrades, though the injustice committed against us was great. I want the reader not to forget that in the United States—boasted citadel of democracy—we were prisoners for opinion, under a fascist-like thought control act. Our imprisonment was a disgrace to our country, not to us.

What happened to us was in no way comparable to the terrible fate of our comrades abroad, the martyred Czech Communist leader, Fuschik, or the French Communist editor, Peri—both executed by the Nazis. But that does not minimize the shame of such laws as the Smith Act, the McCarran Act, and the repressive anti-labor Taft-Hartley and Landrum-Griffin Acts. While they remain, what happened to us and worse can happen again and to many others, non-Communists as well as Communists; workers for peace, Negro rights, union demands. That is why we believe our cases must not be forgotten. But of this much has been said and written, and I will continue to do so elsewhere. Here, rather, I have wanted to tell the human story of a women's prison.

When the women in Alderson learned that I was a speaker and a writer, they would say eagerly, "Write all about this place when you go out, Elizabeth." One pleaded with me just before I left: "Don't forget us. Tell the world about this place." I promised I would. If I can stir up some real interest especially among women's organizations, as my friend Kate O'Hare did years ago, I will not have spent time there in vain. The very young, the sick, the penniless, and friendless, cry out for help, especially to other women. Imagine an old woman who had no place to go, no one to go to; who at the end of a long sentence cried with fear and asked to be allowed to die there. It was her only home. They had to keep her till they found refuge for her, in some other institution. What price prison? If the women's organizations that sponsored the building of Alderson would realize how much it falls short of the original purposes, they would at least insist on reinstating the decent, sensible, and humane procedures of Dr. Mary Harris.

I know I have not been able to do full justice to the subject. If I could be as graphic and persuasive as it demands, it would cause these organizations to insist that it be closed down as inadequate and useless, in fact a school for crime. The women there, in the main, need hospitals, sanitoriums, rest homes, training schools, psychiatric treatment—not a prison. Cut off from the world, from families and friends, denied a chance to earn a living, to learn anything useful, left there to rot, that is the fate of the long-termers. Guarded by untrained women, who are often indifferent, disinterested, disdainful of the inmates, who are in no way fitted for their tasks, what can bloom in such an atmosphere but decay? Possibly the criticism will be made that I am not "objective," a favorite word in the lexicon of social workers. I am on the side of the inmates. If the officers are dissatisfied or unfairly treated, they can walk out. The inmate must accept the place and the treatment. There is no out for her. She does not even dare to speak out.

It is difficult, practically impossible, to learn the facts by investigations of committees and the like. Even ex-inmates are unwilling and afraid to talk. They fear reprisal if they return to the prison, and the FBI and the law's long arm outside. Some of the women in Alderson would say to me: "Be careful. They'll give you a bad time if you tell the truth about this place."

When Betty Gannett was released she made a valiant attempt to have Alderson investigated. She felt so deeply the inhumanity of the place that she was moved to try to do something about it. After she came out, in September 1956, she spoke at gatherings, especially of women, on what she had seen and how the inmates are treated. She visited the veteran Socialist leader, Norman Thomas, who had signed an amnesty petition for us. She was not appealing on our behalf, she told him, but felt that she should do something about the impermissible conditions. He suggested she see Senator William Langer, who was a member of the Sub-Committee on National Penitentiaries, of which Olin B. Johnston was Chairman. He wrote to Senator Langer, who called Betty and made a date for her to come to Washington to see him in November 1956.

However, now she struck a snag. She was under Supervisory Parole with the Immigration Department which refused her permission to go to see a U.S. Senator, who had requested her presence. She went regardless and spent all afternoon with Senator Langer. In the course of their conference, his secretary came in to say: "Mrs. Tormey, there are two men outside with a camera. They say they are from the Department of Immigration and they insist on taking your picture." Apparently they wanted evidence to establish that she had violated her parole restrictions. Senator Langer was indignant and called General Swing, head of Immigration.

He emphatically asserted, "I asked her to come," and explained that she was there as a witness for his committee. General Swing asked to speak to the two men on the telephone and told them to go back to New York City.

Senator Langer explained then to Betty that he would give her a formal witness voucher signed by Senator Johnston, and that her fare would be paid for the trip. In a short time General Swing appeared in person. He apologized to Senator Langer, but explained, "We have to keep on top of all Smith Act people." When Betty Gannett returned to New York City she received an official letter from the New York office of Immigration granting her request to go to Washington and asking her to disregard their former letter. So red tape is preserved!

The next act was a receipt of a letter addressed to Mrs. Tormey, from Francis L. Van Dusen, Judge in the U.S. District Court of the Eastern District of Philadelphia, requesting her to come to Philadelphia and enclosing a letter to the Immigration Department for permission, which this time was immediately forthcoming. He said he wished to discuss "a matter of great importance to the administration of justice in the federal courts." He had been designated to go to Alderson to investigate conditions there and to report to the committee in Washington. He went to Alderson some time between January and May 1957, when he sent her a copy of his report. I was still in Alderson at that time and would have been very willing to talk to him. But I never heard of, nor saw, this visitor. Apparently he talked only to the staff, which is natural. The average inmate would be afraid to talk freely, while still there or facing parole. As was to be expected, Betty's criticisms were denounced and her proposals rejected by the smug ladies in charge of Alderson. Under-officers would no more speak out in criticism than would the inmates. Their jobs would be at stake.

In a personal letter to Betty, Judge Van Dusen remarked: "The staff's reaction to you and your friends was that you never repented of the criminal activities of which you were convicted and showed no disposition to stop them on your release. If this is true, it is hard to blame them for reserving the privileges and rewards for those who did repent and showed a disposition to cease criminal activities when they returned to their home communities." So the Alderson staff became judges of our future activities! This certainly disposes of any charge that we were discriminated against by admitting that we *were* and deliberately so.

He said in the letter that he had not mentioned the subject of "homosexuality because you had no information on it except unspecific hearsay." Father Kerrigan, with whom he had a long talk "was certain that very little of it had taken place and that it had been properly corrected." Naturally Betty did not have knowledge as either a witness or a participant, nor did I. But if her information was rejected as "hearsay" Father Kerrigan's should be likewise. He did not live in the house with forty women nor hear them talk or witness the many suggestive actions in the living rooms or at work. He knew only what inmates or staff told him and they would naturally be reticent on such a subject with a priest. If he had any direct knowledge it would be through the confessional and he would not want to violate its confidential nature.

The one inmate to whom Betty had referred the committee, Judge Van Dusen said, was "unavailable, either because she had locked in or was at church." By the time of his visit, especially as she was to be released soon, she was probably frightened. However, he passed judgment on her as follows: "The staff at Alderson has proof of behavior on her part, which is a good deal worse than anything with which you are familiar." That settled her.

He dismissed Betty's references to Dr. Harris and her humane rules: "It had less than 100 inmates and the situation was clearly far different than it is today. . . . The Reformatory is a place of punishment, having many persons of sub-normal intelligence, as well as rehabilitation, and cannot be run like a normal educational institution."

In reply to Betty's criticism of the placing of young, innocent, first offenders with older inmates, he makes this comment in his report: "The position of the Bureau of Prisons is that the creation of a separate institution or camp for 14-½ or 15 year old girls is not needed in the federal system as much as additional prison facilities for men." In referring to the two young girls from Pennsylvania who were in orientation with us in 1955, he states, "they had been frequent violators of the criminal law prior to their arrival in Alderson." Old hardened criminals, indeed!

So Betty Gannett's attempt to reform Alderson's practices fell on barren soil. A visit of one day or two by a federal judge resulted in a whitewash for the place and an implication that she was a liar—as well as an unrepentent Communist. I have given this episode in full because it illustrates the futility of expecting any change from the Bureau of Prisons, the prison staffs or federal judges unless there is an exposure of such magnitude that public opinion is aroused. It also anticipates the replies that may be made to this book, since I too am an unrepentant Communist and an ex-convict under the notorious Smith Act. I expect slander, abuse, and downright lies to be levelled at me in attempts to discredit what I have written here. I am prepared for this and I hope my readers will be. Of the thousands of women who have passed through Alderson only a handful would dare to speak out and corroborate the truth I have told. No officers, with many of whom I discussed all the subjects in detail, would dare to admit such conversations. Inmates and officers alike are victims of deep fear.

Many charges were made by inmates of graft, of smuggling things into the prison, of dope going in, and what not. But I was not in a position to verify any of these, though I would not be surprised if they were true. I have written only what I know and heard.

The lack of proper medical care and the inadequate protection of an inmate against violence are notorious in all prisons. The death of William W. Remington in Lewisburg Penitentiary, the assault on Robert Thompson, Communist leader, in the West St. House of Detention, are examples. Thompson's skull was fractured by another prisoner, armed with an iron bar, who struck him from behind while standing on the food line. The assailant was a fascist, held for deportation. He said he thought he would be freed if he killed a Communist. The prison habit of characterizing those who complain of illness as malingerers, undoubtedly caused more than one death in Alderson. In the case of Henry Winston, a Negro Communist leader, imprisoned in Terre Haute Federal Penitentiary, his requests for medical aid were ignored until he was unable to walk and going blind. An operation in an outside hospital disclosed that he was suffering from a brain tumor, which had destroyed the optic nerves. Today he is totally blind. The amount of damage this tragic happening alone has caused to the prestige of the United States throughout the world is incalculable.

I have heard from a prisoner recently released from Alderson prison that there have been some changes; transfers and resignations of officers, and retirement of others. But they do not affect the estimation I have given here of the personnel. I was glad to hear that the Christmas carols were reinstated after Miss Bowman left for Terminal Island,[1] and also that a Christmas project was introduced to make clothing for poor children in the area. On the other hand, the music appreciation period had been abolished. The craft shop and commissary were moved to the lower campus, into a new building. Cottage 27 was renovated to receive inmates, as the number in 1960 was 620 and going up steadily. There were 75 in orientation then. The recreational officer was trying to have the basement of the educational building opened as a Recreational Center, as it had been years ago. A man was put in charge of diet and the inmates say it is better. The Indian girl, who had a life-sentence, now works on the farm. Re-classification has been cut down. Formerly, one could apply for a change in job and it was considered by a committee. Now it is very difficult to change one's work. It is evident that the tightening up process, so evident when I was there, has continued.

In conclusion, I wish to point out to the reader there were certain difficulties in writing this book. I have refrained from mentioning names, except of top administration officers. If I were to identify the compassionate officers and those who were friendly to me, they might lose their jobs. If I mention inmates who may still be there or may have returned, they too could suffer reprisal for friendship with me. So I have had to maintain anonymity in these cases. Nor can I mention library books I particularly enjoyed, lest they be removed as "subversive." This may make me sound a bit of a typhoid Mary, but such are the facts of prison life. To be treated with courtesy and consideration, as a friend and an equal, by either inmate or officer, was a breath of fresh air in a fetid atmosphere. The least I can do in return is to respect and protect them. I treasure their memories. In writing this book, I have tried to fulfill my obligation to the women prisoners in Alderson. If I have helped them, I am not sorry I was No. 11710.

As for my feelings when I left Alderson, the following excerpt from a letter I wrote to Kathie a few days before I was released expressed them:

"Nothing and nobody can take my country away from me. I sit in prison, thinking of its beauty, its breadth, its people. It is ever in my heart, my thoughts, my eyes—its growth, its vastness, its richness. Sitting in the twilight, watching the sun sinking in the West, I remember my country, clear out to the Pacific Ocean—over 3,000 miles from border to border—her rivers . . . Hudson, Delaware, Allegheny, Mississippi, Colorado, Columbia; her cities . . . Boston, New York, Philadelphia, Pittsburgh, Chicago, Denver, Seattle, Portland, San

Francisco; her mountains . . . Pike's Peak, Shasta, Mt. Hood, Rainier, Mt. Tamalpais. I remember the drying Salt Lake, the incredible blue of Crater Lake; Mountauk Point and the turbulent Atlantic; Puget Sound and the vast Pacific. I see again the Redwood forest, the Gulf of Mexico, the red earth of the Mesaba Range, the Great Lakes, Niagara Falls, New England in the fall, the snows of Minnesota, even the hills and trees are beautiful here in this obscure corner of West Virginia.

"I love my country and her varied people and I know them well. For over fifty years I have traveled back and forth across the broad bosom of my country, to make it a happier, more peaceful, more prosperous place to live in for our people—children of pioneers, pilgrims, immigrants—all colors, races, religions, origins; I know its poets and its fighters for freedom—Socialists, IWW's, Communists, builders of unions, strike leaders, political and labor prisoners; I know its potentials for a full life, in science, technical skills, know-how; I know its capacity for courage and knowledge; I take pride in Americans—a basically kind, good, generous people."

I returned in July 1957 to meet them again, to travel again, to speak and to write again, to carry the message of peace and Socialism for our country—in my time. To this purpose my life is dedicated.

1. Miss Gladys V. Bowman later returned to the Alderson institution to become the warden.

Appendices

Prison Poems

SUNSET

A Mood in Cottage 26

(Published in Eagle, *Easter 1956)*

The slanting rays of golden sunset slowly move
Across the strange, bare street within the prison.
Here are no sounds of casual traffic, no friendly homes, no
    laughing children,
Only the shrill, sad voices of women are heard afar,
Moving, controlled, upon their daily appointed tasks.
I sit behind a window, barred and screened,
And gaze upon this sterile world of grief, of hungry hearts;
Of shattered lives, of hopes deferred, of anguished love.
But opposite my window, two red peonies stand, erect and
    tall,
Full-petalled, blooming, swaying poised and free,
The sun's rays gently kiss them, a long good-night.
The prison fades a little; their beauty fills my heart.

COMMISSARY LOVE

(Published in Eagle, *Easter 1956)*

I love you more than words can say!
Are you soon going Commissary way?
To you I always will be true,
Yes, the yarn I want is navy blue.
To me you're always fine and dandy.
Be sure to bring me bars of candy!
You surely know I am not lazy,
The cookies you brought me were *crazy!*
For you I'll always sweat and toil.
Oh, yes! I want some hair oil.
Answer me please, don't drive me loco!
All I want is a can of cocoa.
You want my friendliness I hope,
So don't forget some bars of soap!
I never found such a loving friend.
What? Your money's drawing to an end?
Girl! What you say? Sorry, I can't wait!
I've got another friend in cottage eight!

A VISIT FROM AN OLD FRIEND

(Published in Eagle, *Easter 1957)*

Tonight a beam of light jogged my shoulder,
I turned, and the half-moon winked at me.
His plump yellow profile smiled a crooked wicked smile,
And his light shone on the mountains, through the trees.

Ah yes, he smiled and nodded, like a jolly old friend,
Returned from a journey far away.
He said: "I'm here, Elizabeth, I always will be here,
To cheer you on your journey, come what may.

"Together we saw ravished war-torn Paris,
And beautiful San Francisco, all alight;
On the Arizona desert, I was with you,
You glimpsed London from the sky, by my pale light."

In one day's course he visits far-off Asia,
On the broad African lands, his light's ashine;
His face reflects to us this whirling planet.
And promises tomorrow's sun, to climb.

"It's a date," he said, "remember! Count on me!
Nothing and no one can take me away from you.
No bars, no darkness, no prison walls can stop my ray,
Nor blot out the stars, the planets and the Milky Way."

And as he disappeared around the mountain top,
He laughed: "I'm off my myriad friends to see,
When e'er I come I'll bring you messages of cheer,
And I'll light your way to freedom, never fear!"

VENUS OVER ALDERSON—
NEW YEAR'S, 1956

(Published in Eagle, *Easter 1956)*

It is early evening; the sun sets in a red-gold glow,
From my prison window I drink in its beauty.
Behold now, a long hanging planet—"Venus, my shining
    star," a poet said.
Bright, steady, glowing, moving westward
Slowly downward across the sky, following the sun.
It pierces through the delicate, lace-like branches
Of a still-leafless tree outside my window.
Glorious, ageless star, alone in the sky.
Venus, named for the Roman goddess of Love;
The same beautiful one the Greeks called Aphrodite.
Second in order from the sun, in the arch of the Heavens;
Looking upward at you—my spirit soars free.
Star of Women, shedding your light on all of us tonight,
Happy women in bright homes, preparing evening meals.
Here, ever sad women, in this place of sorrow and shame,
Cast the comfort of your radiant rays on us, in prison!
On mothers longing for their children; wives for their mates,
    children for their mothers.
Here, where we slowly count the days, the months, the years;
Following one dreary round of monotonous tasks to the weary
    end.
Faithful and steady, shine your brilliant light into our lonely
    rooms;
Beautiful Star, dipping now to the mountain's edge;
Suddenly you are gone! Leaving a darker sky, but a sure
    promise
You will return tomorrow, Star of women, tomorrow and
    tomorrow, to light our way home.

HOUSEHUNTING IN ALDERSON

(Published in Eagle, *July 1956)*

"The early bird catches the worm," the proverb attests,
No doubt it's the truth that is told,
But the early bird also finds old nests
Deserted and empty, but snug in the cold.

Suddenly they're here, at the first smell of spring;
Robins and sparrows, 'peckers and 'jays,
From far away places they come home on the wing,
Greeting each other on these warm sunny days.

What a flying around! What a mad, ceaseless chatter!
As they compare views from one nest to another;
This one is too low near the loud kitchen clatter,
"Yes, and too near the cats," chirps the anxious bird mother.

They hunt them in trees, water spouts and in eaves.
Will the old nest still do? Does it suit their own way?
Or must they rebuild, of straw and soft leaves?
They decide and move in at the close of the day.

Night falls, and their cheerful cheeps slowly decrease.
Soon will come morning and their new life begins,
Tucked away in their nests they find quiet and peace,
A long happy summer to our free, feathered friends!

ANY ALDERSON HOLIDAY

(Published in Eagle, *Easter 1957)*

Rub-a-dub-dub! Three gals at a tub!
One washing, one rinsing, one tired of waiting,
And some busy scrubbing, their sad fates berating!
While others are ironing, dusting and waxing,
Their voices climb higher, the work is so taxing!
Where's the soap? Where's the starch? Say, that is my sock!
Hurry up, everybody! I'm watching the clock!
Where's the pail, where's the mop, who's got the buffer?
I'll kill you! Drop Dead! If you knew how I suffer!
The steam rises up and the tin washboard creaks.
It belongs in a museum with the other antiques.
A scorched smell from the iron brings forth a loud groan.
A voice asks so plaintively for a cigarette loan.
Oh, heavens, I pray that this holiday ends!
I'm losing my reason along with my friends.
But with assignments all checked and our labors all done,
Comes the solace of card games—we're friends, everyone.
Peace descends on our cottage; our holiday is past.
We look forward to morning and a work day, at last.

MY LITTLE PLANT

(*Published in* Eagle, *Christmas 1956*)

I had a delicate little plant which grew within my heart.
    I nurtured and 'tended it faithfully;
I gave it all the sunshine my soul could impart,
    I watered it with my tears so tenderly.

But it refused to thrive, it wilted and declined,
    Try as I would, I could not make it grow,
'Till finally, in anger, I tore it from its roots,
    And flung it far, to die beneath the snow.

After many days, in sorrow I returned,
    No trace I found, but in my heart I felt its roots astir,
What could I do, I ask, but let it grow again?
    My stubborn little plant that would not die of cruelty
      and pain.

TO THE PRISON MADONNAS

(Published in Eagle, *Christmas 1956)*

Was it a fleeting passion or a deep abiding love?
What matter now, to these tragic, waiting women,
Who sit around a work table in the Craft Shop,
Misshapen, big with child, awaiting their hour of deliverance.
Some sad-eyed, some smiling, talking softly of their hopes and
fears.
Sewing on baby garments, making tiny shoes, passing the days,
'Till "unto her a child is born," within these prison walls.
Does she fear for the little one, sleeping beneath her heart?
Be not ashamed, mother dear, that a child is born in prison!
A Babe was laid in a manger who became the Light of the
world.
A Babe was born in a log cabin who freed a people from
slavery.
Hold good thoughts for your baby to be brave and kind and
true.
Who knows to what heights of human service this baby may
aspire.
Who is now solace for your heartbreak, fulfilment of your
dreams?

SUBLIMATION

(Published in Eagle, *Easter 1957)*

When first one enters this strange lonely place
    Pain, dull and dreary, gnaws at the desolate heart.
Stripped of one's pride, shorn of one's name and space,
    The mind is empty and the soul a thing apart.

But nature gives an anodyne for grief, an opiate for pain,
    That fills the mind with what there is at hand,
Blots out the distant life, the ways of home,
    Lest from the deadening impact one could not withstand.

The vine cut down shoots out new tender roots,
    The severed plant throws forth an anguished strain;
Thus does the human heart reach forth from friendly soil,
    It needs must turn from death-in-life to life again.

To heal the heavy heart, to still the seething brain,
    As days pass by the here-and-now becomes the real,
The world outside grows dim, the present must sustain,
    One strives to keep one's vision, to live by one's ideal.

But sometimes strange and alien poisons seep into the veins,
    In this strange atmosphere of intimate restricted lives,
Where variety is missing, where noisy bedlam reigns,
    Strong emotions grip us filled with horror and surprise.

Contempt, disgust and anger, foreign to one's very being,
    Frustration, boredom, loneliness and oft-consuming hate.
Amazed and alarmed, one must overcome this baser self,
    Restore one's heart to normalcy, calmly accept one's fate.

The constant daily struggle not to sink in a morass,
    To sublimate the primitive unto a higher plane,
To keep one's soul inviolate—"Defeat" one must never say,
    To "Do unto others," and be kind—this is the only way.

CALENDAR OF IMPATIENCE

(Published in Eagle, *Easter 1957)*

Days! Days! Days! So many days to go.
    Count the days, so many more to stay.
Count the days, creeping along so slow,
    Laugh or weep, they still must pass away.

Ever the bright and beaming sun comes up at dawn,
    Ever in splendor sinks at even' time.
Ever the darkness passes, a new day is born,
    Ever the stars and moon across the sky do climb.

But ever the word is "days"—by night and day,
    At meals, at work, on the steps, it is days we sigh,
Good days, meritorious days, industrial days, we say.
    "When will I get my days?" is ever the cry.

The days grew long and summertime was here,
    The many colored leaves announce the fall.
The days grow short as winter's snows appear,
    But "Spring is never far behind," we now recall.

Finally, our days are gone, we gladly know.
    Time rolls on, the seasons pass along.
Outside the gate, into the world we go,
    In our hearts is home, on our lips a song.

But can we soon forget those we left behind?
    Their tears and sorrow, loneliness and pain,
Ever their voices sounding in my mind,
    Bringing their oft-repeated sad refrain,

    "Days! Days! Days!"

FAREWELL TO CLAUDIA

(October 24, 1955)

Nearer and nearer drew this day, dear comrade,
When I from you must sadly part,
Day after day, a dark foreboding sorrow,
Crept through my anxious heart.

No more to see you striding down the pathway,
No more to see your smiling eyes and radiant face.
No more to hear your gay and pealing laughter,
No more encircled by your love, in this sad place.

How I will miss you, words will fail to utter,
I am alone, my thoughts unshared, these weary days,
I feel bereft and empty, on this gray and dreary morning,
Facing my lonely future, hemmed in by prison ways.

Sometimes I feel you've never been in Alderson,
So full of life, so detached from here you seem.
So proud of walk, of talk, of work, of being,
Your presence here is like a fading fevered dream.

Yet as the sun shines now, through fog and darkness.
I feel a sudden joy that you are gone,
That once again you walk the streets of Harlem,
That today for you at least, is Freedom's dawn.

I will be strong in our common faith, dear comrade,
I will be self-sufficient, to our ideals firm and true,
I will be strong to keep my mind and soul outside a prison,
Encouraged and inspired by ever loving memories of you.

A FRIEND

(To Claudia, June 1956)

The longer you are gone, my dearest friend,
The harder are the lonely days to bear,
Eight months have passed—and you so far away;
I have no one my thoughts and dreams to share,
I long to hear your laughter, ringing free,
I long to see your warm and pleasant smile,
To hear your words of comradeship to me
As your swift hands flew at the loom, the while.

Your days are marred by sorrow at my fate,
My days are solitary and they harder grow,
But we can hope—the dawn is never late,
And we will meet again, dear friend, I know.

WALLS

(June 1956)

Walls that shut us in and walls that shut you out,
    That separate the minds and hearts of friends.
Family and life, dreams, joys and hopes they flout
    But like a nightmare, all this too will end.

I know if love could cast down walls, like Jericho's
    Were shattered by the great Joshua of old,
These walls would crumble and their dust would blow
    Far, far away—forgotten and untold.

ON PRISON BEAUTY

(April 1957)

I did not know that I loved freedom so,
Until I lost it in a prison,
I did not know that I loved beauty so,
Until I found it in a prison.
A little rabbit bounding through the snow,
A bright-eyed chipmunk on the search for food,
A mother skunk, four babies in a row,
Are joy and comfort here.
Nature ignores a prison,
Her rhythmic seasons come and go,
Her buds unfold, her tender leaves and blossoms grow.
A tree in bloom, its perfume heavy in the spring air,
The cheerful birds at dawn and dusk,
The crescent moon and star close by,
The rolling mountains fold on fold,
Their distant colors—blues and grays, purple and gold,
The age old rock wall over the green river,
The glory of the rising and setting sun,
Encircles us with breathless wonder.
Nature abhors a prison,
She surrounds us with her beauty like a cloak.

HOW I LONG TO SEE A MAN
(*Spring 1957*)

How I long to see a man, a particular man!
To see him smoke a pipe, a cigar or cigarette!
How I long to talk to a man, a particular man!
About the Elections, the Dodgers, Khrushchev's speech,
The Supreme Court, Nasser and Nehru,
How I long to hear that man laugh, a deep hearty laugh,
Crinkling his Irish blue eyes,
How I long to see his tall frame, his wavy white hair,
His easy walk, his ready smile,
As he walked proudly down the prison corridor when last I
    saw him,
How I long to see that man once again!
Eugene Dennis

How I long to see a man, a particular man!
See his powerful shoulders and giant frame loom through a
    crowd;
See his all-including smile, his beautiful dark face, his gleam-
    ing eyes,
How I long to hear his deep melodious voice say, "Hello,
    Elizabeth."
How I long to hear his glorious singing voice in "Let My
    People Go" and "Meadowland,"
How I long to be enfolded in his comradely embrace;
How I long to sit beside him on a platform, hear his thunder-
    ous words of peace and justice,
Moving me and all who hear to tears of joy.
Paul Robeson

TO VINCENT VAN GOGH

(*Spring 1957*)

You look down upon us from the crafts shop wall,
From a charcoal copy of a "Self Portrait"
Made by one like yourself—a distraught but talented inmate,
Who had known pain and sorrow in a prison.

Your keen and sunken eyes look down upon us,
Your models were like us—the poor, the outcasts, the for-
    saken,
The old, the toil worn, weary and discarded,
In contrast to the beautiful earth, the golden fields of Arles.

Few here know who you are, great artist of the lowly,
They glance unseeingly at your square and homely features,
Absorbed in their own lives, troubles and tasks,
Yet, like a patron saint, you are there, a symbol of us all.

Their stories are in yours and yours in theirs,
The hopes long crushed, the loves betrayed, the self-respect
    denied.
The ambitions thwarted without friends or future,
Their tragic tales unfold, like yours, the end foretold.

Yet from their groping hands come colors, shapes and fabrics,
The creative urge is born, beauty creeps into their souls,
Justifying your faith and love of people,
Though but a small spark of your hot burning flame.

In my memory I see your pictures once again,
Plain people, like yourself, the Old Woman, the Potato
    Eaters,
Miners, weavers, farmers, your fellow artists and above all,
The yellow fields, the blue rivers, the shimmering sunlight,
    the green trees.

Their beauty glows alive to my mind's eye,
Your sorrowful life brings pity for all here,
Your dedication to your work, not to be swerved or stopped,
Calls to like courage in one's duty, unto death.

2

On The Declaration of Independence

(Published in the Eagle, July 4, 1956)

One hundred and eighty years ago, the Continental Congress was assembled in the State House of Pennsylvania at Philadelphia. Its members had been elected by thirteen American colonies—Massachusetts, New Hampshire, Rhode Island, Connecticut, New York, New Jersey, Pennsylvania, Delaware, Maryland, Virginia, North Carolina, South Carolina, and Georgia.

At this time the Colonies were at war with Great Britain. The territory they occupied and claimed was only 829,135 square miles, extending from the Atlantic to the Mississippi and from Canada to Florida. The rest of the North American continent was virtually an unexplored wilderness.

The members of the Congress had come on horseback or by stage coach to represent the United Colonies, and on July 4, 1776, they adopted a Declaration of Independence. It was first published in the *Pennsylvania Evening Post* of July 6, 1776, signed by John Hancock, President of the Congress, and Charles Thompson, Secretary.

Hancock wrote in an exceptionally large and bold hand, "so the King would be sure to see it!" This resulted in the origin of the expression when one is about to sign a paper, "Put your John Hancock there!"

By August all the Colonies had agreed on the Declaration's

adoption and embossed copies, such as we often see printed, were sent to each of the United States of America, the name of the infant government. In the original copy, the first letter of all the important words was capitalized, which was the literary style of that day.

The hall where the Congress met was known thereafter as Independence Hall and is now a national museum, housing among other historically treasured mementos, the Liberty Bell. In 1776 this symbol of freedom was hung in the steeple and pealed out the glad tidings of the bold and brave decision. It bears on its rim the Biblical words: "Proclaim liberty throughout all the land unto all the inhabitants thereof!" A copy of the Declaration was sent by special messenger to General George Washington, then in command of the American Revolutionary Army in New York City, who read it to his troops on July 9, 1776.

There were many famous signers of the Declaration of Independence including two who later became the second and third presidents of the United States, John Adams and Thomas Jefferson. Benjamin Franklin, who wisely remarked at the time, "We must all hang together or we will be hung separately," was also a signer. The Declaration was prepared by a Committee, under the direction of Thomas Jefferson. The Congress was representative of the two million population, as it was then estimated. The signers included farmers, soldiers, lawyers, merchants, physicians, a printer, a brewer, and an iron manufacturer, a college president, and a musician. Forty-eight were American-born, two from England, two from Scotland, three from Ireland, and one from Wales—a total of fifty-six.

Since the passage of the Stamp Act by the British Parliament in 1765, which was rejected by the Colonies as "taxation without representation," they had been in revolt. The Boston Massacre, when British soldiers fired on the people, added fuel to the fires of freedom. The Continental Congress was formed in 1774, and in April, 1775, the American Revolution began with the battles of Concord and Lexington in Massachusetts. In the next seven years, in spite of many defeats, untold hardship and suffering, an heroic and tremendous struggle resulted, and victory and independence were finally won.

The Americans had the sympathy of liberty-loving people around the world, and were aided by the French, represented by Lafayette; the Polish, by Pulaski, and many others.

The purpose of the Declaration of Independence was twofold; to weld the people of the colonies into one whole, as one country, with one over-all national government, instead of thirteen separate states, and to express to all mankind their common purpose and the justice of their cause. It sets forth in detail in sixteen paragraphs, their many grievances against the British tyranny. In language of burning indignation, it indicts the King, George III. This section has served as a model ever since to many colonial and oppressed people seeking independence and self-determination.

It has been echoed in similar declarations by the people of the Philippines, Puerto Rico, Viet-Nam, Algeria, Ireland and many others. But even more inspiring and historically important were those three paragraphs setting forth the new revolutionary, political principles which animated the American people.

After ages of human slavery, feudalism, and absolute monarchies, it was a clarion call for the democratic rights of men. Its guiding principles should be studied and cherished by each succeeding generation of Americans. On the 4th of July, all should read and consider well these immortal words: "We hold these truths to be self-evident that all men are created equal, that they are endowed by their Creator with certain inalienable rights, that among these are Life, Liberty and the Pursuit of Happiness. That to secure these rights, governments are instituted among men, deriving their just powers from the consent of the governed. That whenever a new form of Government becomes destructive of these ends it is the right of the people to alter or abolish it, and to institute a new government, laying its foundations on such principles and organizing its powers in such form as to them shall seem most likely to effect their safety and happiness." They then submitted the facts to a candid world, in the body of the document. The concluding paragraph was their declaration. It reads as follows: "We, therefore, the Representatives of the United States of America, in General Congress, assembled, appealing to the Supreme Judge of the world for the rectitude of our intentions, do, in the name and by the authority of the good people of these Colonies, solemnly publish and declare, that these United States are, and of right ought to be free and independent states; that they are absolved from all allegiance to the British Crown, and that all political connections between them and the state of Great Britain is and ought to be totally desolved . . . and for the support of the this Declaration, with a firm reliance in the protection of Divine Providence, *we mutually pledge to each other our lives, our fortunes and our Sacred Honor.*"

That courage and fighting spirit should inspire us today. Succeeding generations struggled to implement this declaration in life, as in the Emancipation Proclamation of Abraham Lincoln in 1863, declaring the slaves forever free, and in the 19th Amendment to the United States Constitution, passed in 1920, giving suffrage to American women.

The Bill of Rights, the first ten amendments, was added to the Constitution in 1791 to specify the rights of the people and to reserve to the people powers not delegated or prohibited by the Constitution. It is a logical conclusion of the Declaration of Independence. These are not just historical documents but lasting guarantees. It is our duty to safeguard and protect them, and to practice their principles, in all our domestic and foreign policies. It would be well for every American to read again on each 4th of July, both the Declaration of Independence and the Bill of Rights, to refresh our memories of their immortal words, to cherish our democratic traditions and to practice them in life.

1. Freedom of Speech and Expression
2. Freedom of Religion
3. Freedom from Want
4. Freedom from Fear.

Organizations in Washington Conference, 1923

These 21 organizations participated in a conference in Washington, D.C., in September 1923, which adopted a resolution recommending: (1) That a federal institution to house federal woman prisoners be established; (2) That it be placed near the geographic center of the prison population; (3) That its capacity provide for 700; (4) That the institution be described as a "Federal Farm for Women"; (5) That the minimum amount of land be 500 acres; (6) That the institution be built on the cottage plan to permit of classification; (7) That the head of the institution be a woman.

American Association of University Women
American Federation of Teachers
American Home Economics Association
American Prison Association
American Social Hygiene Association
Bureau of Home Economics
Daughters of the American Revolution
Democratic National Committee
General Federation of Women's Clubs
Girls' Friendly League
Lumen Femina, W.T.A.
National Committee for Mental Hygiene
National Committee on Prisons and Prison Labor
National Congress of Mothers and Parent Teacher
    Associations
National Council of Women

National Council of Jewish Women
National Federation of Business and Professional
    Women's Clubs
National Women's Christian Temperance Union
National Women's Trade Union League
Republican National Committee
Women's City Club, Washington, D.C.